Louder Than Words

GW00383651

'Dietrich Bonhoeffer stressed "theology is a helper, a support in the struggle not an end in itself". In this tradition Andrew Bradstock brilliantly feels the pulse of faith concerns in early twenty-first-century Britain. Read it to catch up and together we can tackle future challenges.'

John Battle MP

'Within the Pentecostal churches there is a tradition of holiness that underpins a call to service in the world. The prophet Amos offers us an example of what such service means and Andrew Bradstock points the reader in the direction a twenty-first-century Amos would take.'

Nims Obunge, Pastor of Freedom's Ark Church and
Chief Executive of the Peace Alliance

'This is both an inspirational and thought provoking read and an instrumental reference book. It explores big picture twenty-first-century issues and brings you right down to earth with relevant and helpful action points. An essential read for the thoughtful activist. Andrew Bradstock has really done his homework.'

Joy Madeiros, Director of Public Policy, Faithworks

'Andrew identifies some of the key issues confronting today's world and gives valuable practical tips on applying our faith to these. The analysis and solutions he offers will provoke a useful debate, and his commitment to applying faith to political and economic problems is a powerful example to us all.'

Paul Woolley, Director, Theos

'*Louder Than Words* is a book of wide scope that dares to dream the "possible". Bradstock carefully outlines many contemporary issues that challenge the world today, climate change, HIV/AIDS, poverty and asylum and encourages action by people of faith by articulating hope. The role that Christians may play in influencing public opinion, in changing personal lifestyles and campaigning are seen as a passionate call to living faithfully in the world. If as Bradstock suggests Christians in Britain must now earn their place in the public sphere, his book not only demonstrates why this is so necessary but also serves as a handbook for how to go about it.'

Anthea Cox, Co-ordinating Secretary, Public Life and
Social Justice, The Methodist Church

Louder Than Words

Action for the 21st-Century Church

Andrew Bradstock

DARTON · LONGMAN + TODD

First published in 2007 by
Darton, Longman and Todd Ltd
1 Spencer Court
140–142 Wandsworth High Street
London SW18 4JJ

ISBN-10 0-232-52610-9
ISBN-13 978-0-232-52610-3

A catalogue record for this book is available from the British Library.

Phototypeset by YHT Ltd, London
Printed and bound in Great Britain by Page Bros, Norwich, Norfolk

Let justice roll down like waters,
and righteousness like an ever-flowing stream.

Amos 5:24

The soul of religion is the practical part ... at the day of doom it will not be said, Did you believe? but, Were you doers, or talkers only?

John Bunyan, *Pilgrim's Progress*

Never doubt that a small group of thoughtful committed citizens can change the world. Indeed it's the only thing that ever has.

Margaret Mead

Contents

Foreword

Jubilee 2000 was an international campaign whose main drive and energy derived from the dedication and commitment of Christians. Many thousands made sacrifices, worked voluntarily and without recognition to raise an immensely important issue to the top of the global political agenda – and bring about a change in the balance of power between powerful creditors in rich countries, and weak debtors in poor countries. The impact of their combined voices and actions continues to ripple through the global economy, as more and more countries like Nigeria, Argentina and Brazil pay off their debts in advance, and regain some independence from foreign creditors.

Initially many believed that a movement of ordinary people could not achieve such change. At the beginning many were doubtful that matters of international finance and economics were matters that they could legitimately grasp, and influence. Many people questioned whether their faith obliged them to do so (only to be quickly reminded by Ched Myers and others of the centrality of debt to the Lord's Prayer and of Christ's preoccupation with matters of money, finance and economics.) Even more people feared that these were issues of such complexity, that they would not be taken seriously. With the help of expert briefings and educational talks, these fears were gradually overcome, and many thousands of ordinary church-goers educated themselves in matters relating to international finance and debt. They then used their understanding to enormous effect – bringing intense pressure to bear on officials and politicians in both governments and international institutions.

For those of us involved in the campaign, this was its most inspiring element. Ordinary people came to realise that the thing they feared most was not their weakness, but their power. That by linking up with others, by remaining united, focussed, dedicated and principled, they could exercise power beyond measure. This astonished Jubilee 2000 supporters. Above all it astonished and shook the powerful – politicians, officials and the media – who were taken aback by the breadth and strength of Jubilee 2000's support; by the depth of knowledge and understanding of the campaign's supporters – and by their motivation and determination.

Andrew Bradstock draws on the lessons of the Jubilee 2000 and Make Poverty History campaigns and provides people of faith with the intellectual and campaigning tools they need to play a part in transforming our world into one that is sustainable, peaceful, equitable and just. This book is a valuable and timely resource. It surveys all the major areas of current political debate, reviews the key issues, and helps readers go deeper: to discover books, briefings, information and points of entry into campaigns. It is a generous book, acknowledging the contributions of a range of actors and agents in diverse campaigns and organisations – and giving the reader the wide range of information needed to make sensible judgements.

Above all it is fired by the conviction that people of faith can play a vital role in transforming our world, whether it be at global or local level, by making the links between their faith and social and political action. Andrew tackles the difficult issues of intolerance and racism confronting communities in Britain; of the need to build bridges within and between faiths; and between faiths and their communities. But he also urges action that will alter the trajectory of events at a global level: on the environment, war, terror and poverty.

This book inspires, leads and instructs. Above all it is a practical route map for those serious about applying their principles to worldly affairs. It will help many to rise to the challenges facing us all.

Ann Pettifor

Preface

The idea for this book arose while I was Secretary for Church and Society with the United Reformed Church, a post which enabled me to work at the front line of the churches' engagement with the issues discussed here. Although I had previously taught academic courses on the churches' involvement with current issues, made visits to the developing world, and actively supported aid and environmental agencies, it was only as I began to work 'behind the scenes' with these agencies and with figures from government, the global institutions, business and other faith traditions, that I really understood the potential that churches have to make a difference in the world and, indeed, to help to build a better one. Within the United Reformed Church I had opportunities to share this vision at all levels of the church, and I hope that through this book I can spread it further.

I make no apology for this being a passionate book, though I hope it is also an informed and realistic one. The experience of serving on the boards of Jubilee Debt Campaign and Stamp Out Poverty (formerly Tobin Tax Network); of helping to found and develop 'Just-Share'; of being in at the start of Make Poverty History and helping to launch it in the churches; and of representing the United Reformed Church on numerous networks, committees and projects, gave me not only inspiration but also a grasp of the issues we confront and a realistic assessment of what is 'possible'. If this book has a large canvas (not least in proportion to its size!), it is because I believe we should not be afraid to engage with the big issues of our day, nor doubt that we can have an impact on them. We know in many cases what is needed to achieve change: we need the faith, perseverance and strategies actually to bring it about.

It was an honour to serve the United Reformed Church as one of its secretaries and a stimulating experience to work with its Church and Society Committee under its Convener, the Revd Martin Camroux, and with the Commitment for Life team led by Anne Martin. I owe a special debt of thanks to my colleague Wendy Cooper, upon whose vast knowledge and wisdom in church and society matters I needed constantly to draw. Visits to Christian Aid projects in Jamaica and Mali and with the Amos Trust to Nicaragua had a profound effect on my understanding of development issues, as did regular meetings with people from the major agencies, not least over those breakfasts at No. 11!

It is a privilege to work with many people at the front line of the issues discussed here, and I am profoundly grateful to those who have been kind enough to read and comment on sections of this book. Each has put her or his expertise at my disposal and helped in many different ways to improve the text (though final responsibility for it is of course mine). So my thanks to Michael Bartlet, Francis Davis, Dr Elizabeth Harris, David Hillman, Steve Hucklesby, Jon Kuhrt, Rt Revd Stephen Lowe, Joy Madeiros, Alun Morinan, Martin Pearson, Revd Dr David Pickering, Janet Quilley, Stephen Rand, Jo Rathbone, Tim Reith, Revd Peter Southcombe and Revd Sally Thomas. I am also grateful for the input and suggestions for improvement I have received from Ellen Armstrong, Phil Baldwin, Revd Annis Fessey, Canon Brian Fessey, Richard Stainer and Dr Wilf Wilde, and from those who attended events where I shared some of my initial thinking – including the Greenbelt Festival, seminars at Westminster College, Cambridge and University of Durham Theology Faculty, and a conference of the Modern Churchpeople's Union. I have greatly enjoyed working with my editor at Darton, Longman and Todd, Virginia Hearn, whose enthusiasm for this project and professional advice have been crucial to its completion. I also thank Ross Shimmon for help at the proof-reading and indexing stage. Finally, my special thanks to Terry Drummond CA, who has been with this project since its inception, given me regular doses of encouragement and wise counsel, and, not least, read and commented on the whole manuscript.

I dedicate this book to my wife Helen, whose love and inspiration mean so much to me and who shares my passion for a just and peaceful world.

Andrew Bradstock
Ash Wednesday 2007

Chapter 1

Introduction
On actually making the world a better place

Let us love, not in word or speech, but in truth and action.

1 John 3:18

'Truth and reconciliation' read a banner headline in *The Independent* in November 2006, backed by harrowing scenes from 'The Troubles' in Northern Ireland over the preceding 35 years. The story inside told how an IRA volunteer, who had spent 16 years in the Maze for an attack on a military billet, and a Belfast Protestant who had seen his family killed by an IRA bomb, had been secretly meeting with a former British soldier to 'talk about the past, with the aim of creating a better future'. It was a gripping and inspiring report, stressing how those involved wanted to recover and deal with the painful truth of their history and work at the dialogue for as long as it took. It also described how the initiative – named 'Healing Through Remembering' – had drawn inspiration from the South African reconciliation process overseen by Archbishop Tutu. The report also mentioned that the 'former British soldier' had become an ordained Anglican priest and was working with the Church of Ireland.[1]

Here was an uplifting tale in its own right but also a 'good news' story about religion – a break from the usual portrayal of faith as a malign, even murderous phenomenon whenever it manifests itself publicly. On its own, this story could hardly correct the negative image of religion often promoted by the media, but it did give a glimpse of the *positive* impact that people of faith can have on contemporary issues and the contribution that churches and other 'faith communities' can offer towards making the world a better place.

This book is about the way that churches are working to create a more just and peaceful world. It takes the issues that challenge us most today – hunger, climate change, war, terrorism, social tension – and explores what churches are doing to bring about change and how we can make our impact even greater. It is concerned not so much with *whether* Christians should be involved in re-making the world, but more with what we are doing to make it happen and how we can do it more effectively.[2] Believing that the God we encounter in Scripture is concerned about human affairs, this book asks, How can God's desire to see justice and peace prevail be met in our world today? How can *all* truly know the 'life in all its fullness' that Jesus came to announce?

The need for action
As its title suggests, what drives this book is the need for action. It really says no more, but also no less, than: this is what we've achieved; this is what we still have to do; the goals that we have *are* worth pursuing; and here are some practical steps we can take towards reaching them. In specific terms, it argues that the vision of eradicating child poverty, of slowing global warming, of rebuilding trust in our communities, of turning swords into ploughshares *can* be realised if we work together, adopt clear strategies and sustain our faith that the changes we are struggling and praying for *are* possible. This book suggests that a vision of a 'better world' is not something we should be ashamed to have as Christians – indeed, it surfaces time and again in Scripture; but the book argues that the challenge is to let that vision inspire us as we try to live out our faith, aware, in the beautiful words of Teresa of Avila, that God has no body, hands or feet on earth but ours. The twin convictions behind this book are that, not to act in the face of the enormous challenges we face is to have a faith that truly is dead (Jas. 2:17); and that, important though what we say and confess as Christians undoubtedly is, it will be by our practical commitment to re-making the world that our religion will ultimately be judged. The Digger leader Gerrard Winstanley put it well when he reflected that 'words and writing [are] all nothing, and must die, for action is the life of all, and if thou dost not act, thou dost nothing.'[3] At a time when religion is being subjected to unprecedented scrutiny, actions really do speak louder than words.

So this is essentially a practical, down-to-earth sort of book – though being thin on 'theory' does not mean being thin on *theology*, since we learn about God as we live out God's commands and reflect on that experience, something strongly encouraged here. But I confess to being more concerned in this book with the 'how' of changing the world than the 'why'.

So what am I proposing?

Tackling climate change

The biggest threat to our survival as a race is global warming, an issue which we have become increasingly committed to tackling. The enormity of this threat demands nothing less than a wholesale change in hearts and minds – among politicians, business-people, the media and the wider population – since only a radical shift in our individual and collective behaviour will pull us back from the brink. As Christians we can play an important role in raising awareness about the issue, both in our local communities and at a wider level, and this book suggests that we should not only promote a 'greener' lifestyle (by word and by deed), but also help to effect such a transformation in our culture as to make the political action that is needed inevitable. In the manner of the prophets of old, we should be unafraid to say the things that people find uncomfortable to hear, including about the impact that our behaviour has both on the environment and on poor communities in the developing world. Believing that they offer a realistic way forward, I also suggest that we continue to promote initiatives like the 'contraction and convergence' programme, which seeks to achieve a significant reduction in greenhouse gas emissions in a way that plays fair by the world's poorer nations. There is much that we can do as churches in our local neighbourhoods to make a real and lasting difference, and a range of actions with potentially long-term consequences is suggested here.

Terror and war

If climate change is the biggest spectre haunting us this century, the others are war, terror and poverty. Unlike climate change and poverty, the 'war on terror' and the propensity of nations to engage in war may seem beyond our power to affect, yet there is much that we can do as we seek to follow Jesus' challenge to be peace-makers. In the face of an apparent reluctance by governments to try to uncover and deal with the roots of terror, we can lobby politicians to allocate resources, not just to target terrorists but also (to quote Jim Wallis) to 'drain the swamp of injustice around which the mosquitoes of terrorism breed'. As churches we should also challenge the bad theology and inadequate frames of reference that underpin the so-called 'war on terror', and seek to feed into the debate the more radical – and workable – model of national security found in scriptures like Micah. I also highlight here the vital contribution Christians are making towards healing the deep and painful divisions caused by war, and towards building for a more peaceful future, noting in particular some of the imaginative work being done in Bosnia, Uganda, Israel/Palestine, Iraq and Northern Ireland.

Global poverty

That 50,000 people continue to die every day from hunger or preventable diseases is an evil we have sought to overcome for decades, and we have an impressive track record as churches through the work of our various aid agencies and significant roles in both Jubilee 2000 and Make Poverty History. But in many churches, involvement in Christian Aid or Tearfund or SCIAF is still something that only a few committed people 'do', or a focus for just one week or one Sunday in the year. In this book I suggest ways in which we might radically alter our churches' thinking on this. Seeing the Millennium Development Goals – with their target of massively reducing poverty and improving opportunities for education and health care in the developing world by 2015 – as a sign of commitment by the global community seriously to tackle these issues, I argue that we must sustain our pressure on world leaders for action on debt, trade and aid, as well as support fair trade and those campaigns which press politicians to find 'new money' for development. The key to actually 'making poverty history' is a commitment by world leaders to do just that – and that is a challenge we must not ignore.

Nearer to home

Debt, child poverty, low wages and exploitation are not only 'third world' phenomena – they occur on our doorsteps as well. Here in the UK we have a target to see child poverty eradicated by 2019, and we should press for an all-party consensus around this goal so that any change of government does not imperil progress towards it. Again, there is scope for churches to be prophetic on this issue, and there are sound Gospel reasons why we should be among those expressing concern about the growing inequalities in our society and calling for a narrowing of the gap between rich and poor. I suggest we should also continue to highlight the plight of people seeking asylum in this country as well as migrant workers and people who have been 'trafficked' into Britain – for example, for the sex industry. Finally, I note the opportunities that now exist for churches to help transform their local communities and the people and families that those communities embrace.

Building bridges

A further important contribution we can make as churches to our local situations is to reach out to people of other faiths. In the wake of the 7/7 bombings, hostility towards Islam has increased in many quarters – helped in part by some irresponsible and uninformed reporting and commentary in some sections of the media – presenting us with a challenge to seek to foster better relationships with Muslims and people of other faiths in our communities. Initiatives like twinning our church with the local mosque, promoting space for dialogue and conversation, and working together on local projects, are all ways we might explore of helping to break down fear and misunderstanding and healing fractured communities. I also suggest that there is vital work we can do in terms of raising levels of understanding about religion among opinion-formers and shifting the terms of the debate, noting that so often the language in which discussion about faith issues is couched – with repeated use of terms like 'extremist' and 'fundamentalist' – is inappropriate, unhelpful and potentially dangerous. Finally, I look at other, more general ways in which churches can facilitate dialogue as a way of promoting greater understanding and harmony within our communities and society at large.

Being specific

A number of convictions inform this book. First, I believe we must be *specific* and *positive* in what we say and do. For a long time many of us in the churches have banged on about creating a 'just world', 'transforming sinful structures' and 'building the kingdom', without really explaining what we meant by these terms or how the changes we wanted were to come about. I am not suggesting that we have been wrong to speak out against those things we have discerned to be harmful, immoral or sinful in our world, but I do believe we have not been good at articulating what we have wanted in their stead. Being denunciatory, or presenting simplistic answers to complex social and economic problems, can suggest laziness or naivety; it also fails to impress the politicians whose minds we seek to change, and whose response to generalised statements about values is always 'How does this cash out in terms of hard policy?' Being prepared to accept a compromise is also something which we may find difficult but which may be necessary if real change is to be secured.[4] If we want to engage meaningfully in the business of making the world more just, we must accept that there are no short-cuts to wrestling with the issues and offering realistic, workable strategies. By way of example, in Chapter 2 I cite a plan that was drawn up by churches in the USA as an alternative to the invasion of Iraq – a model of a practical, realistic programme to augment a protest against what they saw as an immoral policy.

Tackling the roots

Secondly, I believe we need to tackle the *roots* of the evils we confront, not merely the symptoms. I guess there are few of us now, within or without the churches, who still think that giving money is a sufficient response to situations of need, given what we know about the mechanisms that keep people poor. While at one time we might have done little more than give to our favourite charity, now we have a basic understanding of how global trade rules operate against the interests of developing-world farmers, how servicing unpayable debt impacts on the infrastructure of poor countries, how our buying Fairtrade goods can benefit producers in those countries, and how lobbying and direct action can achieve real political change. Whether the issue is peace, or poverty, or the environment, or social cohesion, the emphasis throughout this book will be on identifying and treating the deeper issues, with the aim of achieving lasting rather than temporary change. Was not the point about the Hebrew concept of 'Jubilee' – even if it was never tried – that it envisaged a situation where poverty was actually eradicated and, with it, the need for what we used to call 'Christian charity'?[5]

Central to this will be the need to challenge 'received wisdom' – those 'norms' which are often unthinkingly accepted but which will have to shift if change of the kind we envisage is to happen. Often we get lulled by opinion-formers into thinking that something is 'inevitable' or an unalterable part of the way things are, when in fact alternatives *are* possible if we are prepared to think deeply and critically. As we have noted, many of the prophets of old did this within their communities, often with powerful effect, and Jesus himself made almost everyone he met reflect deeply on their own and their society's values. In confronting the huge issues of our day, we also need to be prepared to speak and act 'prophetically', and in this book are some suggestions of ways in which we might challenge popular wisdom about, for example, the ever-widening gap in our society between rich and poor, the inviolability of our comfortable lifestyles in the face of climate change and global poverty, the contribution that people of different faith traditions can make to our society, the necessity of a 'war on terror', and the importance of tackling situations of conflict at their roots.

Believing we can ...

Thirdly, we must never lose hope that the changes we are struggling for *can* be achieved. It is easy, when confronted by the enormity of the situation we face – the pace of global warming, the scale of attacks by terrorists, the sheer number of people living in dire poverty and/or with HIV/AIDS and/or in countries ravaged by war – to despair of things ever improving. When factors holding back progressive and just solutions are added in – inactivity or dissemblance on the part of some governments, the self-interestedness of some multi-nationals, corruption and malfeasance in high places, what Ephesians calls 'the principalities and powers of this present darkness' (6:12) – our pessimism and sense of inadequacy can become even greater. Yet these are actually exciting times in which to be pursuing social change, because we know what is needed to achieve 'a better world' and it is within our capability.

When we listen to senior politicians talking about how the threat of climate change or the spread of HIV/AIDS can be overcome, they all admit that the key factor is not cost or resources but 'political will' – by which they mean a commitment by world leaders actually to make change happen. It is disturbingly evident, whenever governments decide to engage in or prepare for war, that money and person-power can be found for causes they deem serious enough, even at very short notice. The challenge for us is to persuade governments that they should demonstrate the same level of commitment – indeed, *a much higher level of commitment* – to protecting the environment and overcoming hunger as they do to military exploits. On one level,

this sounds a tall order, given that more than a million of us pro-
testing against the invasion of Iraq did not convince our Prime
Minister to change his decision.[6] But the key is to commit to the 'long
haul', to work at what Jim Wallis has called 'changing the wind', so
that eventually politicians can no longer ignore the force of our
argument.[7]

I do think this is hugely important. Wallis often talks about how
politicians fear to act unless they know they have popular backing,
how they always need to discern the way the wind is blowing and
then move in that direction. We should of course expect a degree of
responsiveness to public opinion on the part of elected representatives in democratic states, but it is the case that legislators more often
follow the public mind than seek to shape it. Hence political change
can be achieved as we work to raise public awareness and shift public
opinion, as we change the culture in which our political leaders
operate. And the reason I see our present moment as one of great
opportunity is because church people are good at helping to 'change
the wind' and have an impressive track record to prove it.

The issue of developing-world debt is a case in point. At the
beginning of the 1990s few people were aware of how significant debt
was as a factor in perpetuating poverty in developing countries, yet
by the year 2000 – thanks to a movement founded by two people with
the genius to link the issue to the 'Jubilee' principle in the Hebrew
Scriptures – a massive, unstoppable campaign was capturing the
imagination of millions throughout Europe and beyond, demanding
that all outstanding debts be 'dropped'. Those of us in the crowd of
70,000 lobbying the G8 leaders in Birmingham in 1998 will never
forget the experience, yet one of the most striking things about that
event was the proportion of campaigners who were from churches (in
some cases whole congregations seemed to have turned out), and this
had a major impact on the media and the world leaders gathered for
that summit. Neither could dismiss the lobby as a 'rent-a-crowd'
event, for many of the people there were engaging in street action for
the first time, driven simply by their passion for the issue.[8]

Without the support of churches, church-based agencies and
individual Christians, 'Jubilee 2000' would not have been the wind-
changer it was. Much of the impact it made was down to Christians
giving sacrificially of their time and money and building grassroots
support in their churches and neighbourhoods, plus faith-based
agencies producing first-class resources, the Christian media covering

the issue in depth and church leaders speaking out. And it is no exaggeration to say that Jubilee 2000 did 'change the wind', for not only can it point to achievements that have transformed the lives of millions of impoverished people in the developing world, but also it has made the issue of debt so high profile that world leaders dare not exclude it from their agenda whenever they meet. Much the same could be said of 'Make Poverty History' in 2005 which, again with massive support from the churches and Christian agencies, not only inspired millions to campaign and march to see poverty ended, but also secured some impressive commitments from the G8 summit in Edinburgh.

Mountains *do* move

The fact is that revolutions *do* still happen, and church people are often at the centre of them. However impossible the odds against overturning injustice can appear to be, with patience, resolution and faith huge mountains can be moved and radical and lasting change can be achieved. The ending of apartheid is a particularly powerful example of this, being won after many long years of sacrifice, protest, lobbying and boycotting by millions inside and outside South Africa, including church people. Against seemingly hopeless odds, they remained steadfast in their conviction of the 'just-ness' of the cause and committed to fighting for as long as it took. The abolition of the slave trade two centuries earlier provides another case in point, being championed by Christians and others who, again after decades of tireless effort, achieved a gradual breakdown of 'accepted norms' to create a situation where reform was unstoppable. The mountain they faced must have seemed as insuperable as some of those we face today, but their faith succeeded in moving it after literally a lifetime spent 'changing the wind'.

These campaigners, together with figures like Elizabeth Fry, Josephine Butler, Martin Luther King and others who devoted their whole lives to fighting injustice, can be models for us as we struggle to see poverty eradicated, our environment protected and alternatives to conflict prevail. Like these earlier campaigners, a conviction that we are pursuing God's priorities will inspire and inform our action and enable us to persevere, even when the hour seems darkest and the temptation to give up is strongest. Our conviction that God's purposes ultimately win through will only strengthen our resolve to make them a reality.

But we can't do everything

Yet conviction, enthusiasm and passion are not enough to alter prevailing winds on their own, which is why this book discusses, not just a vision of a better world, but policies and programmes that will make it happen. It does not claim to offer an exhaustive list of policies, nor to explore issues in intricate depth, since it does not seek to appeal primarily to experts. Its aim is rather to show how, as thinking and informed people in the churches, we can make a real difference in our world. To this end, it offers a range of possible actions which individuals, groups and churches can choose to adopt, according to their capacity, together with website addresses and further reading for those seeking more information on specific points.

Struggling together

It is nowhere assumed in this book that one person or church can do everything suggested (though it does highlight connections between the different themes addressed and how the action we take can impact on more than one issue). Its underlying conviction, of course, is that change is achieved as we work together through agencies and networks devoted to particular concerns. The importance of our contribution as individuals and churches is therefore strongly affirmed, for while we can often get dispirited and wonder what 'one person can do', seeing our action within the context of wider national and even global movements will help to encourage us not to give up.[9] The Church of England's Lent initiative for 2007, which encouraged church members (via text messages) to undertake small actions to help 'spread generosity and happiness in their community', operated on this principle. As the archbishops of York and Canterbury said in its support, 'It's all too easy to feel we are powerless to make a difference, but the truth is, with God's help we can change the world a little bit each day.' This very much reflects the spirit informing this book.

The idea that what we do as individuals or small groups will never make much difference can be refuted by many inspiring stories about 'small beginnings'. In the mid 1990s, for example, a group of women with no educational background and very little money founded (after a hard-fought struggle to secure a licence) a bank in their region of India with the aim of helping other Indian women to develop small-scale enterprises. In its first ten years the Mann Deshi Mahila

Sahakari Bank (MDMSB) created 17,000 women entrepreneurs in the region around Mhaswad and transformed the lives of many thousands more women, children and men. Nearer to home, in the 1980s a group of people at St Ives Free Church in the Fens began selling fairly traded goods from a trestle table at the back of their church – an initiative which, within ten years, had led to the church converting some of its space into a shop that was open six days a week, employing the equivalent of two paid staff and turning over £55,000 per year. Not only has this venture helped transform the lives of many producers in the developing world and raised awareness about fair trade in the local community, but also any surpluses made have been used to benefit other projects in various parts of Africa. (It is also probably the only business ever to have held a party to celebrate needing to register for VAT, having proven its success by hitting the £50,000 annual turnover threshold!)

On the question of collaboration, while we may prefer working with agencies which have a faith basis or motivation wherever possible, we should also be open to partnering with those which do not, realising that the issues are too important for us to adopt a 'purist' or 'isolationist' mentality. One of the lessons of the parable of the sheep and the goats in Matthew 25 is that among our allies in the struggle for the kingdom will be those who, while not explicitly acknowledging Christ as saviour, practically demonstrate God's passion to see justice prevail. Yet if we have to recognise that, as Christians, we cannot make the kind of impact we want to on our own, we should also reflect that no major changes in the realm of poverty reduction or protecting the environment will be possible *without* the committed involvement of people of faith. The challenge made by Gandhi that we should 'be the change that we wish to see in the world' – also used by the archbishops to support their Lent initiative – underpins this book, for it is clearly insufficient to campaign or lobby for fairer global trade or a reduction in carbon emissions if we do not live consistently with these aspirations.

A spiritual struggle?

The emphasis on action in this book should not hide the fact that we need *spiritual* resources for our struggle. In challenging us as Christians to sustain or increase our commitment to fighting poverty and working for peace, I am not seeing prayer, fellowship and Bible study as 'optional add-ons' to this activity (in a reversal of more traditional interpretations of the Gospel), nor am I encouraging churches to replace their weekly schedule of preaching and worship with lectures on the environment or letter-writing sessions for Amnesty (though doing this at other times would be great!). Rather, I am reflecting a reading of Scripture that understands following God to be about belief and action – or 'faith' and 'works', as the writer of James has it – and seeking to pay special attention to one side of that equation.

My argument, in other words, is that the Bible does not suggest that God is to be found purely through disengagement from the world or through worship, prayer, fasting or contemplation alone: active obedience to God's commands is also essential. Knowing God can be equated with 'judging the cause of the poor and needy' (Jer. 22:16), and some of the Old Testament prophets even went so far as to say that worship not offered within the context of a commitment to justice and righteousness is an offence to God.[10] Our social action will therefore not be an 'extra' to our faith but the very essence of it, sustained by, and in turn resourcing, our regular practice of prayer, study and worship. As Christ found time, amidst a life of extra-ordinary activity and service, for prayer, retreat and solitude, so we will – much more so – need times of refreshment, including fellowship with others of like mind, to encourage and inspire us in our task. And if our struggle for a more just world really does involve taking on the 'principalities and powers', then undergirding it with prayer will be imperative: indeed, insofar as they are about achieving justice, valuing the human, fighting for others rather than self, all the struggles described in this book have a strong spiritual dimension which we ignore at our peril.

Action as evangelism

Action is also not proposed here as an alternative to evangelism or the wider task of 'mission'. As David Bosch has pointed out in his seminal study of the subject,[11] since Jesus came both to bring us salvation through his death and resurrection *and* to provide us with a life to follow, proclamation and social action are both essential components of mission. Many churches may define the Gospel almost exclusively in terms of Christ dying for our sins, and see their primary task as preparing people for the world to come, but Jesus' calling was to announce God's imminent reign, a kingdom of reconciliation, peace and new life. Authentic mission therefore entails both proclamation and, as Ann Morisy has put it, 'journeying out' to 'embrace strangers, work for social peace and justice and partake of God's gracious gift of salvation.'[12] Indeed, since the Gospel offers the possibility of transformation and regeneration at the level of the personal as well as the social and structural, it could be said that proclamation and social action both also constitute evangelism.

Recovering the kingdom

Putting a greater emphasis on action within the life of the Church will mean recovering a focus on 'the kingdom'. As Christians we have a natural instinct to see the survival of our churches as our *raison d'être*, whereas the Gospels suggest that Jesus and his early followers were less passionate about setting up and maintaining institutions than transforming people and inaugurating God's dynamic reign of justice and peace. This is not to suggest that we should be relaxed about the possibility of our churches dying, but if our calling is primarily to be 'kingdom people' rather than 'church people', we must at least be open to finding new expressions of church in order to follow that calling faithfully. Engaging more actively with the issues of our day will signal our recovery of the vision of the Church as an essentially outward-looking, serving community over against a more static institution concerned primarily with itself and its own well-being.

What would it mean to make the kingdom our focus? We have become used to the idea of the reign or kingdom of God as a spiritual, even post-mortem entity, but on the lips of Jesus it clearly embodied a hope for the transformation of *this* world. He lived and taught a radical new way of being – one which privileged the poor and the outcast, challenged attitudes towards money, possessions and status, and demonstrated love for others even to the extent of laying down his life – and he calls us to follow him. Rooted as it was in values which were not 'this-worldly' (John 18:36), Jesus saw the kingdom as already among us, challenging accepted norms at the individual and collective levels and positing new and liberating ways of being. Much of the 'world-changing' nature of Jesus' message has been lost by the Church over the centuries, not least as it has made itself comfortable with the world as it is, but the original genius of the kingdom lay in its power to inspire us to want to see it impact radically on our world. We can never complete the task of building the kingdom – it is, after all, the 'kingdom *of God*' – but if we could recapture something of its original power, our passion to overcome injustice, work for peace and welcome the stranger would be all the greater.

The end of Christendom

Another reason why action should become our priority relates to the changing status of the Church in our society. As we have just observed, for more than 1500 years Christianity has enjoyed enormous privilege, power and influence in the West and has massively helped to shape its culture and institutions. During this 'Christendom' era the Church has been listened to – and obeyed – largely on account of its status and close alliances with the 'powers that be', but now there are signs that this era is ending and that the Church will have to compete with other voices for the right to be heard, a right we will earn by backing up what we say by what we do. Being *authentic* is what matters today, and only as we demonstrate a consistency between what we teach and how we live will we be seen as 'believable'. As Stuart Murray, a leading writer on the Church after Christendom, has suggested, earning the right to be listened to may involve, for the Church, reprioritising 'mission' over the maintenance of institutions and putting our emphasis on achieving social justice rather than preserving social order. The Church, he contends, may need to rediscover what it means to operate at the margins of society with a vision which focuses more on prioritising the powerless than exercising power itself.[13]

It is indeed salutary to note that, at a time when religious issues are on our front pages and there is widespread concern to understand what motivates people of faith, our churches are still perceived largely as concerned with their own internal structures, with their freedom and 'right' to operate as they wish, and with a narrow range of what have been traditionally defined as 'ethical' issues. As this book highlights, many in the churches have adopted a broader ethical agenda which encompasses poverty and environmental concerns, but as a whole the Church is far from being seen as a body that is passionate about making our world a better place – and therefore a credible institution deserving a wider hearing. It has also, of course, become much more used to exercising power itself, and seeking the change it wants through the wielding of that power, rather than the example that Jesus showed of speaking truth *to* power.

As Christians we are also aware how much 'bad' religion there is abroad at the present, from the highly toxic variety which sees indiscriminate killing and bloodshed as justifiable in the pursuit of a 'greater good', to the socially impotent kind which understands God's interest in the world to extend only as far as rescuing souls for heaven. As a reaction to the former, some commentators argue that 'religion' should be put in its place, practised in private by consenting adults but not allowed to have influence in 'the public square'. Our answer must be to promote 'good religion', recognising the inherently public nature of the Gospel as lived and taught by Christ, and seeking to live it out in ways that challenge structures built on injustice and discrimination. At a time when religion is under such close scrutiny and subject to much uninformed criticism, it is vital that we show the inherently life-affirming and liberating power of the Christian Gospel.

The vision thing

Finally, a word about vision, which I have highlighted as important but not really unpacked. Having a picture of what it plans to achieve is vital to any programme for change, yet politicians and leaders often avoid any reference to 'vision' because they may not be in office long enough to pursue it or are constantly confronted by immediate crises. Within Christianity, however, vision has always held a central place, and one contribution that we can make to 'changing the world' is to feed into progressive programmes elements of the biblical vision for humankind.

The 'kingdom' is one resource we can offer, its potential to transform both people and communities having already been noted. While it challenges us now to live out its radically different values, it also holds before us the vision, as the American theologian Walter Wink has put it, of 'a domination-free order' characterised by 'partnership', 'interdependence' and 'mutual respect between men and women that cuts across all distinctions between people'.[14] This informs our action now because there is an important and vital connection between our 'living the kingdom' today and its future realisation. The reign of God, in other words, does not just emerge, fully fashioned, at the end of time, but exists in historical continuity with the present. In 'striving for the kingdom' now (Luke 12:31), we both transform the present and build for the future.

The Bible has many other visions upon which we can draw, one of the most beautiful and powerful being Isaiah's depiction of a community where all enjoy the work of their own hands, live out their full life-spans and refrain from hurtful or destructive practices (65:17–25). This picture of all having sufficient for their needs, of harmony between planet and people, and of an absence of discord to the extent that wolf and lamb share the same food-trough, is a deeply inspiring one at this historical juncture. In a similar way, the image of the new heaven and earth envisaged by John of Patmos, in which mourning and pain are also seen as things of the past, can be inspirational (Rev. 21). That John talks in terms of a 'city' is also significant, symbolising as it does a sense of people in community. The Eucharist or Lord's Supper itself, with its strong emphasis on 'sharing in the one meal' and receiving it in equal measure, also powerfully prefigures the spirit of community envisaged in talk of the kingdom and a new heaven and earth.

The whole of Scripture points to a coming 'omega point' in human history, a time when, as Paul puts it, 'the creation ... will be set free from its bondage to decay and will obtain the freedom of the glory of the children of God' (Rom. 8:21). Thus, in addition to the more 'concrete' and immediate actions encouraged in this book, we need to keep 'imagining' the future society – and world – we wish those actions to bring about. But imagination, though vital, is only half the story, for the bigger challenge is to show how our vision is realisable, through the policies and actions that will get us from where we are to where we want to be. If this little book can help us to identify a few of these, and encourage us to believe that it is worthwhile to adopt them, it will have served its purpose.

Chapter 2

War and Terror
Pursuing peace in a troubled world

> Peace is life itself. But by peace I do not mean a life of passivity. I do not mean a life without action because sometimes we have to act a lot to bring about peace.
>
> Aung San Suu Kyi

Jesus' commendation of those who make peace is one of his best-known sayings. Placed by Matthew at the outset of his ministry (Matt. 5:9), it is central to his whole teaching. Admittedly, Jesus is to be found, a few chapters on, suggesting that he has come to bring a sword rather than peace (10:34), but the context suggests that he is anticipating the consequences of his radical, and potentially divisive, call to follow him. From the 'peace on earth' message of the heavenly host proclaiming his birth (Luke 2:14), through his word to the sick to 'go in peace and be whole' (Mark 5:34; Luke 8:48), to his injunction to 'love your enemies' (Matt. 5:44), to his promise to leave his peace with his disciples (John 14:27) and his rebuke of the use of the sword in Gethsemane (Matt. 26:52), Jesus' whole ministry was oriented towards establishing *shalom*. Not for him that mere 'absence of conflict' that we too readily accept as 'peace', that temporary relief from hostility achieved by papering over the cracks or attending just to symptoms. Rather, Jesus calls his followers to seek that deep and lasting wholeness, integrity, well-being and flourishing that comes from overcoming injustice and transforming lives at both the individual and the communal levels.

To say that Jesus' followers have not consistently pursued that kind of peace is hardly contentious. This is not the place to explore or critique the role that the concept of 'redemptive violence' has played in Christian thinking,[1] nor to rake over the coals of the Crusades, the Inquisition, the European subjugation of the Americas or any of the other atrocities done in the name of Christ – except to say that it was not always thus. Before the 'conversion' of Constantine in the fourth century, believers were constantly in trouble for refusing to condone war or be conscripted into the army, and no Christian theologian ever sanctioned participation in war or declared one 'just'. Rules adhered to by the third-century Church even lumped soldiers, 'military constables' and all who 'governed by the sword' along with brothel-keepers, self-mutilators, makers of idolatrous pictures and astrologers as people to be refused baptism without amendment of their way of life.[2] Our challenge today is to recover that commitment to peace-making in order to make a real difference to our communities and our world.

It is often said that peace-making is an active calling: a peace-maker is not someone who merely approves of or demands peace but one who actively works at building reconciliation and removing injustice. Clearly, we will seek to do this within our local communities and neighbourhoods – some of the most challenging contexts for peace-making today – and some approaches to this are considered elsewhere in this book. In this chapter I want to ask how we make sense of Jesus' call at the national or global level. How can we respond to the imperative to make peace today in a world increasingly resembling a global battleground for international terrorists, suicide bombers and a unilateralist superpower and its allies? What can we offer to a world in which 35 people are killed *each hour* as a direct result of warfare, 90 per cent of them civilians and 50 per cent of them children? Do Christians and churches have anything to say to this situation or the resources and commitment to work for peace in ways that are both faithful and effective?

Iraq

The events of the last few years suggest that, despite the record of the Church in centuries past, many Christians today do have the will and imagination to make an effective contribution for peace. The invasion of Iraq, initiated by the governments of the United States and the United Kingdom in March 2003, was unique in bringing all the mainline churches in both countries (with the exception of the

Southern Baptists in the USA) together to oppose it. Whether from a conviction that all wars are immoral or that this one in particular lacked any legal or just basis,[3] churches united against it as never before, turning peace-making – which, bizarrely, had become mainly associated with movements on its fringes – into a concern of the mainstream Church. Never before had a war been so universally condemned by church leaders and members, who were (and continue to be) a significant part of the wider anti-war movement.

One of the high points in the churches' campaign against the war was a series of visits, in the days leading up to the invasion, by a delegation of United States church leaders to the capital cities of the G7 countries. The purpose of these visits was both to strengthen and augment the work of church leaders in the countries visited, and, with them, to lobby the political leadership against waging war. In the UK the delegation met with leaders from the main denominations, Churches Together in Britain and Ireland, and prelates from South Africa and the Middle East, going with them to Downing Street for a 50-minute conversation with the Prime Minister. The church leaders approached this with the intention, not of backing Tony Blair into a corner, but of engaging with him as a fellow Christian and encouraging him to explore options other than war to achieve the removal of Saddam Hussein. The discourse was conducted in terms that recognised the moral and theological dimension of the debates over Iraq, terrorism and the threat of weapons of mass destruction.

This episode confirms the value of the churches having a positive as well as a 'negative' agenda, of them being constructive as well as critical; for while many people marched and spoke out against the war – a necessary as well as very powerful response – the American church leaders brought with them their own alternative plan to bring Saddam to justice without resorting to war. The plan had six points – it became known, predictably, as the Six-Point Plan – and set out to be, in the words of its authors, 'a morally rooted and pragmatic initiative [which] could help achieve an historic breakthrough and set a precedent for decisive and effective international action instead of war.'[4]

The Plan is worth spelling out in full since it demonstrates how a faith-inspired initiative can be both consistent with Christian values and politically engaged. It was also highly original, perhaps the only credible attempt at the time to find (in language used, apparently without irony, in the letter sent with it to the Prime Minister) a 'third way' between war and inaction in the face of the threat posed by Saddam. Its points were, as summarised in the church leaders' message to Blair (which also ran as a full-page advertisement in five British newspapers on the day of the debate in Parliament on the war):

1. Indict Saddam Hussein for his crimes against humanity and send a clear signal that he has no future in Iraq, setting into motion the internal and external forces that could remove him from power and bring him to trial at the International Court in The Hague. History has shown, as with Slobodan Milosevic, that this can help bring down a criminal regime.

2. Pursue coercive disarmament with greatly intensified inspections backed by a UN-mandated multinational force.

3. Foster a democratic Iraq through a temporary post-Saddam UN administration, rather than a US military occupation.

4. Organise a massive humanitarian effort through the UN and non-governmental relief agencies for the people of Iraq now, rather than only after a war.

5. Commit to implement the 'road-map' to peace in the Middle East, with a clear timetable towards a two-state solution that guarantees a Palestinian state and a secure Israel by 2005.

6. Reinvigorate and sustain international cooperation in the campaign against terrorism, rather than having it disrupted by a divisive war against Iraq that intelligence officials believe will likely lead to further attacks.

As we survey, several years on, the tragic hopelessness of the situation in Iraq, the daily news stories of unrest and violence, and the heart-rending death toll of civilians and indigenous and foreign troops, the fact that the churches' Six-Point Plan was not tried may strike us as a lost opportunity. Had its concerns – to give the weapons inspectors more time to do their job, to plan properly for a post-Saddam Iraq, to pursue in tandem a just and lasting solution to the Israel/Palestine situation and, not least, to target Saddam while protecting the Iraqi people – been heeded, how different might things look now in Iraq and beyond. But of course the Plan was rejected by both Bush and Blair, almost certainly – as one of its promoters, Clare Short, has said – because they had already committed themselves to an invasion four or five months before.[5]

Yet this should not lead us to conclude that the project was futile. To seek peace, by definition, requires a preparedness to risk one's venture turning out to be, in purely political terms, ineffective. Even if they had been unable to secure any purchase for it at all, the American churches showed great integrity and courage in seeking a peaceful and just resolution to the situation in Iraq as it was then understood. But in fact they did make an impact, seeing their Plan receive serious consideration not only at the highest levels of government in the UK and the USA but also at the United Nations and in the Vatican. Given its intrinsic merit, and the efforts the church leaders made to see that it received the widest attention, there was every reason to believe, all other things being equal, that the Plan might have informed White House and Downing Street policy towards Iraq.

And that is a point worth underlining, for while this initiative by the American church leaders should be noted simply as a matter of historical record, it should also inspire us as a model which we might want to follow should we hear sabres rattling again in Washington and London during the 'war on terror'. Given heightened American interest in Iran in recent years and bellicose utterances about other countries, there can be few who seriously believe that Iraq will prove to be the only state on the so-called 'axis of evil' that the present Washington administration will seek to 'sort out' militarily. Ought we not then, as people called to be peace-makers, to be among those who not only observe the signs of the times, but are ready with both a word of protest and an alternative strategy informed by a deep commitment to a just and peaceful transformation?

The 'war on terror'

Opposing the military option towards Iraq still leaves questions about our response, as Christians, to the threat posed by global terrorism. We may believe that bombing Iraq was not a justified response for the US administration to make to the events of 9/11; that the effect of invading Muslim countries may be to exacerbate rather than restrain terrorism; and that war is an especially ineffective response to terrorism: but what does it mean to 'make peace' in the context of unspeakable atrocities like the 11 September 2001 attacks on New York and Washington, the 7 July 2005 bombings in London, the Madrid train bombing of 2004 and other acts of terror?

Here we must recognise that, in the face of such an unprecedented situation, we may have no unique insights: at best we simply place our contribution alongside those of other people of goodwill. Jim Wallis, chief architect of the Six-Point Plan, may well be right in his assertion that 'Christian peacemaking is more a path than a position' and that humility is a good trait for Christians when faced with hard questions.[6] Humility is also appropriate as we recall the Church's own historical record and that it is itself caught up in 'the compromises and conflicts of humanity', as a report by a group of Anglican bishops has put it.[7] Indeed, in the sense that we benefit from unjust economic structures which cause millions of unnecessary deaths every year, or are not scrupulous about how our savings, investments and pension plans are invested, we all share some responsibility for war and conflict.[8] Yet we do have something vital to offer in at least two areas: lobbying governments to address the roots and not just the symptoms of the problem; and challenging the language in which the confrontation with terror is conducted.

The importance of tackling the root causes of violence has been highlighted by the World Council of Churches, which has designated the period 2001–2010 the 'Decade to Overcome Violence'. The 'Decade' is not about offering churches 'set programmes' but about encouraging them to do what they can in their own context – though the introductory material does stress the importance within the peace-making process of 'overcoming the systemic inequalities that lead to violence in the first place.'[9] Unpacking what these 'systemic inequalities' might be is a difficult and complex process, but they clearly include poverty, powerlessness and injustice.

It is of course naïve to suggest that terrorism is always a response to poverty, deprivation or inequality, yet it is hardly more realistic to seek to address terrorism while ignoring these phenomena – and Christians need to be among those saying that. In their influential book *Making Terrorism History*, Scilla Elworthy and Gabrielle Rifkind cite evidence to suggest that simply trying to hit back and destroy an enemy serves 'only to increase the level of violence and the chasm between the two sides'. Only new strategies that 'address the full range of factors that fuel cycles of violence and influence the use of terror' – including 'the economic, social and cultural context in which violence is sustained' and 'the emotional and psychological effects of violence and humiliation' – will be successful, they argue.[10] So while our commitment to make poverty history in the two-thirds world may be informed primarily by our belief that poverty is an evil we have the capacity to defeat, we should also be among those encouraging governments to factor into their strategies for global peace the persistence of widespread poverty and of economic and other forms of inequality. The prophet Isaiah speaks to our time when he says that it is integrity that will bring peace, and justice that will bring everlasting security (32:17). A prerequisite for true peace must be dialogue to achieve a stronger concept of justice across religions and cultures.

It has been rightly said that if every single terrorist were arrested and put out of action tomorrow, nothing would be solved until the roots which nurture their activities are also destroyed. There is, as Elworthy and Rifkind have put it, 'no finite number of terrorists in the world to be smoked out, imprisoned or killed. Their numbers are controlled instead by the level of anger and hate that drives people to join their ranks.'[11] Therefore a war on poverty and injustice is every bit as vital as a war on terror: indeed, authoritative figures such as Colin Powell and Gordon Brown have drawn links between the two. Church leaders in the United States have been saying this to their President and we need to be saying it here. If the goal is national security, we need to remind leaders of the intensely practical and contemporary vision of the prophet Micah – in which nations no longer lift up their swords against each other or 'learn war any more', because all their people enjoy the security that comes from being able to 'sit under their own vines and under their own fig trees', with no one making them afraid (Mic. 4:3–4).

Factored into our argument will be the question of how governments spend our money – in particular, the proportion devoted to military projects over against tackling the root causes of injustice. It has been estimated, for example, that the amount that Western governments have spent in Iraq since 2003 would have enabled the Millennium Development Goals to be met already, and the question of whether the UK should renew the Trident nuclear missile system when its lifespan ends in the 2020s also brings the use of resources into sharp relief. As opponents of Trident have pointed out, replacement could cost as much as £25 billion, money which could otherwise be spent on training tens of thousands more teachers, nurses, midwives and fire-fighters, or abolishing student top-up fees for a decade, or protecting 900 million acres of rainforest, or meeting our aid target of 0.7 per cent of GNP every year for six years.[12]

Some church leaders used this argument when Trident came up for review in 2006: an open letter signed by 20 Church of England bishops noted that the costs involved in maintaining and replacing the system 'could be used to address pressing environmental concerns, the causes of terrorism, poverty, and debt'; the Parliamentary Officer for the Quakers, Michael Bartlet, suggested that nuclear weapons were 'hardly relevant against a threat of terrorism' and that investing in them was not 'a rational use of resources in responding to security challenges of the 21st century'; and the Archbishop of Wales called on the government to set a moral example by not replacing Trident, an act which, he said, 'might also encourage us to invest in a wider range of political, cultural, economic and social responses to areas of conflict, threat and need in our world'. These points were made within the context of a searing attack on the Trident missile system *per se*, which the bishops described as 'threaten[ing] long-term and fatal damage to the global environment and its peoples', an end so 'evil' that it made the system's possession and use 'profoundly anti-God acts'. Bartlet also suggested that renewing Trident would violate the Non-Proliferation Treaty under which states already in possession of nuclear weapons agreed to work towards disarmament in return for states not having nuclear weapons committing not to develop them.[13] The Church of Scotland also firmly opposed renewing Trident, and some 30 leaders from the Anglican, Roman Catholic and Free churches signed up to a campaign organised by the Fellowship of Reconciliation in 2006 calling on the government to stop using taxpayers' money to subsidise, through the Defence Export Services Organisation (DESO), the export of arms to areas of conflict and governments which abuse human rights. John Paul II once suggested that within the process of disarmament there is a place for imaginative unilateral initiatives, or 'audacious gestures of peace', with which sentiment these actions would seem to be in accord.

A rather different response to the issue of government spending on the military is to seek to withhold that part of one's tax which is used for waging war and have it redirected towards peaceful and non-military purposes. The intention of those pursuing this objective is not to opt out of their responsibility to society by paying less tax, but to have their conscientious objection to 'paying others to kill on their behalf' acknowledged – a logical extension to the right to refuse to be conscripted into active military service. In the United States the singer Joan Baez led a campaign against paying tax to fund the war in Vietnam in the 1960s, and, in Britain, Quakers have been among the best-known war-tax resisters, some having been tried and punished for their pains. Quakers have been involved institutionally as well as individually, their national representative body, 'Meeting for Sufferings', having, as an employer, challenged government policy in the 1980s by withholding tax on behalf of several staff members at their request. 'Conscience – the peace tax campaign', which is supported by more than 50 MPs from all parties as well as many MEPs, MSPs and AMs, also campaigns for the legal right for those with a conscientious objection to war to have the military part of their taxes spent on peace-building initiatives. A group known as the 'Peace Tax Seven' has been lobbying for a change in the law on the basis that the European Convention on Human Rights, which recognises freedom of thought, conscience and religion, is part of UK law under the terms of the Human Rights Act 1998.

Healing divisions

Addressing root causes within the context of peace-making also involves seeking to heal the divisions between peoples that are caused by or give rise to situations of war. The suggestion that the churches may have a role in post-conflict Iraq in terms of healing division through dialogue has been made by a group of Anglican bishops chaired by the former Bishop of Oxford, Lord Harries. Reflecting upon how lasting democracy might be achieved in Iraq, the bishops raise the possibility of the churches contributing to a public dialogue involving other (mainly Muslim) religious leaders at which an acknowledgement of the way that the West has contributed to the present situation is made. Suggesting as a model the Truth and Reconciliation Commission in South Africa, which was chaired by an Anglican archbishop, Desmond Tutu, the bishops see such a forum providing, not only the opportunity for religious leaders in the West to make a 'mature, public act of institutional repentance', but also space for 'ordinary Iraqi people to tell their stories so that truth-telling can indeed promote reconciliation and healing'. If it is able to bring people at grass-roots as well as leadership level together and, as in South Africa, involve a large proportion of the population, it could, argue the bishops, 'have a significant impact on the creation of a culture of human rights and democratic values.' While the bishops think it unlikely any government would initiate such a process, there is no reason why we should not seek to persuade both our government and our church leaders to pursue it, given the evidence of the South African experience and the palpable need for new and imaginative strategies to be attempted in Iraq.[14]

The work that Christians have done in other contexts to bring warring factions together is also an inspiration. For much of the period of 'The Troubles' in Northern Ireland, staff at Quaker House in Belfast worked patiently and quietly behind the scenes, promoting dialogue between all the parties involved. Drawing upon their positive reputation in the province going back over 200 years and adhering to a fundamentally non-partisan stance, Quakers provided a safe space for the leadership of both sides in the conflict to meet and converse, and built up themselves relationships of trust with these leaders and with the police and the British and Irish governments. Their acknowledged neutrality – which could be witnessed in simple gestures like giving tea indiscriminately to families queuing to see relatives in the Maze – allowed them not only to ask uncomfortable questions, but also to enable key players such as ex-prisoners from both sides to hear each other's stories. Central to the Quaker House philosophy was a commitment to listen rather than 'provide answers', to work out possible ways forward rather than achieve 'targets'.

Similar reconciliation and peace-building work was also undertaken during the 1990s by ECONI – Evangelical Contribution on Northern Ireland – which in 2005 changed its name to the Centre for Contemporary Christianity in Ireland. ECONI has had a particularly important role to play in asking challenging questions of their own Protestant evangelical community. CHIPS – Christian International Peace Service – also worked for peace and reconciliation in Northern Ireland, setting up a mixed 'household for peace' in a troubled area of Belfast. CHIPS has also worked in Cyprus, bringing Greek and Turkish Cypriots together, and in Uganda, where many years of working to reconcile two tribes with a long history of conflict has resulted in members of both tribes living, praying, worshipping and working together.

This kind of commitment to genuine peace-making goes against the grain of our culture, which expects instant solutions to problems and undervalues qualities like patience and persistence. Yet we need to be among those saying that real and lasting peace cannot be achieved through short-cuts, that people and communities cannot be changed unless the pain and suffering they feel and experience are acknowledged and worked through. As Pat Gaffney of Pax Christi has written apropos the situation in Iraq:

> it takes time to discover the root causes of violence and injustice, and it takes time to try to address these through dialogue and negotiation. It is a process of trying to change hearts and minds so that when solutions are found they are lasting and have addressed the underlying injustice.[15]

Renewing the language

As Christians we need to ask uncomfortable questions about the language in which the current 'search for peace' is conducted. This might include querying the very concept of a 'war on terror', given, as Elworthy and Rifkind have rightly noted, that 'terrorism is a tactic rather than a definable enemy'.[16] The United Reformed and Methodist churches have recently argued that 'the terminology "War on Terror" should be resisted because it unhappily slips between the ambiguity of "war" used as a metaphor (such as the "war on drugs") and real wars in which real weapons kill real people.' They note the failure of the war in Afghanistan following 9/11 to apprehend those responsible for that atrocity or suppress the insurgency that followed the overthrow of the Taliban regime, and how in fact it 'provoked widespread anger among Muslims particularly for indiscriminate attacks on villages.' Instead of 'rhetorical myth-making' involving the terminology of war, the churches' report suggests, more attention needs to be given to understanding, addressing and resolving the conflicts that provoke terrorism.[17] The report by a working group of Anglican bishops also cautioned against describing the threat posed by terrorism 'in the language of war', and other commentators have noted how references to a 'war on terror' can easily be heard as a 'war on Islam' and can provoke further war-like responses.[18]

Linked to this, we might challenge the morality of defining people as 'terrorists', a dehumanising term which can help to legitimate the killing or torturing, not only of those whom one believes to be involved in terror, but also of the 'innocent' women, men and children with whom they live. There is also the related question about the moral acceptability of demonising countries by locating them on an 'axis of evil'. As was often asked at the time when this terminology was first used, upon what criteria is such a categorisation made, and what attempt is made, when so defining these countries, to differentiate between their governments, the mass of ordinary citizens and any political or 'popular' organisations that may operate there? Is the use of such apocalyptic terminology intended to do anything other than give moral justification to the invasion of those countries on the grounds that evil is always to be eradicated, and suggest that the invader, by implication, is a force, or 'crusader', for good?

Challenging the theology

Given the extent to which those executing the current 'war on terror' have sought to defend it in pseudo-theological terms, there is clearly a challenge to theologians and others in the Church to offer alternative interpretations of the texts used, not least those in the Book of Revelation. As Michael Northcott has written in his critique of American responses to 9/11, *An Angel Directs the Storm*, while the authorities in the USA use Revelation to justify their 'expansionist' foreign policy, John of Patmos, as a truly apocalyptic writer, actually unveils the real nature of empires and speaks of their ultimate failure and replacement 'by the direct rule of God through the communion of the saints'. Yet the influence of writers and preachers in the USA who define Christianity in terms of private moral behaviour, and look for human redemption in terms of 'individual choice aided by the theoretically autonomous mechanism of the free market', makes any theological critique of US foreign policy or its consequences extremely difficult.[19] The task of recovering a more authentic reading of Scripture is clearly an important one within the context of seeking a truly peaceful resolution to the 'war on terror'.

Then there is the question of how helpful the often casual and unreflective juxtaposition of the terms 'Muslim' and 'fundamentalist' in political speeches and media articles has been towards an understanding of the true nature of Islam and bridge-building between different religious communities. Has it not served mainly to fuel the impression of Islam as an essentially violent and aggressive creed while also (intentionally or otherwise) masking the less than constructive role that some within the Christian tradition have played in situations of conflict in recent years? There is much in the suggestion made by Bishop Harries' group that we should work to promote the terminology of 'orthodoxy' and 'heresy' rather than that of 'moderates' and 'fundamentalists', and that, as churches, we should seek to 'reintroduc[e] journalists and politicians to the need to understand the theological components of fundamentalism.'[20]

Building for the future

While a violent response can only at best bring short-term benefits, genuine peace-making is about building for the future, and there are many examples to inspire us in this work. Corrymeela, for example – a centre in Northern Ireland with explicitly Christian foundations – sets out to tackle the mistrust that has underlain the conflict in that country for the past few decades. Its core belief is that real peace comes only through understanding and reconciliation, and it seeks to enable people – not only from Northern Ireland but from many other countries – to gain the confidence to live together free from fear and suspicion by creating a safe space for them to meet, learn about one another, rediscover each other's humanity and share common ground. A similar project, 'Teaching About the Other', has been initiated with support from authorities in Palestine and Israel to enable children from both communities to understand better each other's religion and hear reasonably unbiased histories of the conflict of which they are unwittingly a part. This is a vision also shared by the Olive Tree Educational Trust which has as its by-line, 'nurturing a shared future for Israelis and Palestinians', and the Centre for Peace, Non-Violence and Human Rights in Osijek, Croatia, which seeks to use dialogue to build bridges between Serbs and Croats. Such projects are worthy, not only of support, but of imitation in the sense that education for peace is something we can all engage in by promoting that inner transformation that enables each of us to see the 'sacredness' of the other. As Abraham Garcia, a Guatemalan victim of torture, has said, 'peace isn't the simple silencing of the bullets. It must be an inner change toward other people, respect for the way they think and live.'[21]

Imagination ...

Finally, being serious about making peace requires a preparedness to challenge accepted norms and seek and pursue alternatives to war with persistence, faith, imagination and courage. Interpreters of the Gospels such as Walter Wink argue that it was this that was behind teachings of Jesus such as 'do not resist evil' (Matt. 5:39) – a challenge not simply to accept their oppression, nor respond violently to it, but to find a 'third way', to 'break the cycle of humiliation with humour and even ridicule'. 'Going the extra mile', for example, was a way of embarrassing the occupying troops and putting them in the wrong because they were only entitled to request assistance for one mile.[22]

Donald Reeves, for many years Rector of St James's, Piccadilly, has spoken of the need for 'moral imagination' in peace-making. Drawing upon the seminal work of John Paul Lederach and his own experience of reconciliation work in Bosnia with his organisation 'Soul of Europe', Reeves speaks of how, when facing situations of conflict, we need to imagine ourselves in a web of relationships which includes the stranger or adversary. Emotional and human responses to violence must be addressed, Reeves argues, for 'when healing in the heart and mind has no opportunities to begin, then sooner or later the cycles of violence will return.' In creating a 'web of relationships', it is also important to discover what Reeves calls a 'critical yeast' (rather than a critical mass), 'a small group of people who in the right places and at the right time can make a difference' by activating the other ingredients. 'Moral imagination' also requires us to pay attention to memory – understanding how the past and present relate to the (shared) future which is being pieced together – and to develop 'peripheral vision', to be open to what may be discovered serendipitously in the pursuit of something else. This radical approach to peace-making, which Reeves has himself tried, is one which Christians in other contexts may consider adopting.[23]

Other examples of creative approaches to ending conflict abound. In Uganda a major breakthrough was made in the long-running conflict when an Anglican bishop told a rebel leader – widely held to be responsible for numerous crimes against humanity – that the 'divine spark' was as much visible in his face as in any other. This gesture – which both re-humanised the rebel leader and diminished the 'demonic' status that others had attributed to him – led to him making a totally uncharacteristic call for peace. In Colombia a community situated right in the heart of a war zone took the difficult and highly dangerous decision not to provide assistance to the army or to any armed groups of the left or the right involved in the country's long-running conflict. This example was followed by more than 50 other communities, with the support of church and human-rights groups, thus having a profound effect in a country that has endured continuous armed struggle since the 1960s.

In the Holy Land some Westerners have been accompanying Palestinians and Israelis in their efforts to end the occupation. Under the aegis of EAPPI (Ecumenical Accompaniment Programme in

Palestine and Israel), these volunteers live for three months alongside local people who have chosen to make a non-violent response to their situation, monitoring and reporting violations of human rights and international humanitarian law, supporting acts of non-violent resistance by local Christian and Muslim Palestinians and Israeli peace activists, offering protection through non-violent presence, engaging in public policy advocacy and generally sharing their experiences and standing in solidarity with the churches and all struggling against the occupation. This work also has a strong educational component in that, upon their return to their home countries, EAPPI volunteers are encouraged to raise awareness about the situation they have encountered.

... and courage

A somewhat more 'risky' accompaniment project was undertaken in the 1980s by groups of North Americans who camped out in areas of Central America then being targeted by the US military. Living and working with local communities, these groups (which typically included significant numbers of Christians) invited, through their body language, their fellow-countrymen to destroy those communities 'over our dead bodies'. This is perhaps the ultimate expression of Christian peace-making, a literal readiness to lay down one's life for others.

Something of this ethos informs the Christian Peacemaker Teams currently in Iraq, whose activities received worldwide attention in December 2005 when four of their number, including retired British scientist Norman Kember, were taken hostage.[24] Much debate has been conducted in the media about the wisdom and effectiveness of civilian peace activists working 'on the ground' in Iraq and opening themselves to the same level of risk as that faced by the coalition forces, but the reality is that such a non-violent approach to peace-making is potentially an extremely positive force for good and another powerful example of the contribution that Christians can make to resolving situations of violent conflict by radical, alternative strategies. By maintaining a continuous presence in Iraq (contrary to their critics' claims, they did not just 'drop into' Iraq but were there well before the invasion in 2003) and earning the respect of local people, Christian Peacemakers are able to help empower them to stand up for their own human rights, document abuses of human rights where they occur, and even, in collaboration with Muslim

Peacemaker Teams, help to build bridges between Iraqi communities that are in conflict. Christian Peacemakers may also have prevented violence against Christians in Iraq by demonstrating that the invasion of the country was not part of a war of Christianity against Islam, an impression which may have been (albeit unintentionally) created by governments in the West. It is interesting that when Kember and his colleagues Harmeet Singh Sooden, James Loney and Tom Fox were taken hostage, calls for their release flooded in from Muslims all around the world.

Prayer and solidarity

Action such as this often lays Christians open to accusations of naïvety, of believing that a non-violent response to aggression or tyranny will always bring it to an end. In some cases, of course, it does, but in others it is the peaceful campaigners themselves who are killed: Jesus was crucified, Gandhi and Luther King were assassinated, Tom Fox was abducted and shot in Iraq. Yet, as the Quaker campaigner Kathleen Lonsdale has written, these visionaries 'did not fail. Nor did they leave behind them the hatred, devastation and bitterness that war, successful or unsuccessful does leave.' No person, group or nation need be ashamed of this method of opposing evil,' Lonsdale writes, in the way that 'we may and should be ashamed of the inhumanities of wars that are perpetrated in our name and with our support.'[25]

Only the few will be called to work as 'accompaniers' or Peacemakers in situations of conflict, and even they will undergo a rigorous selection and training process.[26] But supporting the witness of these people through prayer and solidarity is something we can all do, recognising their willingness to undergo the same risks as those in the military in their search for peace through ways other than armed conflict. They, like the American church leaders with their Six-Point Plan, seek a peaceful resolution to conflict through ways that demonstrate an understanding of the situation confronted, a concern to be constructive, and a consistency with the teachings of Christ. These criteria are important for us all as we constantly hear afresh the Psalmist's challenge to 'seek peace, and pursue it' (Ps. 34:14) – a challenge which needs our informed, committed and creative response as badly now as it ever did.

Chapter 3

Climate Change
Radical action to save the planet

God has made all things in the world in consideration of
everything else.

Hildegard of Bingen

'The earth is the Lord's ... so how should your church respond?' is
the arresting slogan on a leaflet produced by Eco-Congregation, an
ecumenical project helping churches to 'weave environmental issues
into their life and mission'. It's a question that more and more of us
are taking seriously, not least as we realise the severity of the crisis we
face as the planet continues to get warmer. Those of us who believe
that the earth is indeed the Lord's and our calling is to be good
stewards of it, will be committed through both prayer and action to
seeing the crisis averted. But what specifically can we do, as individuals and churches, to help slow down the onset of global warming –
a threat which no less an authority than the government's chief scientific adviser, among others, has described as more serious than
terrorism?

We ought to acknowledge first that Christians have not always
made the link between God's 'ownership' of creation and human
responsibility for its survival. While the celebrated attacks on the
Judaeo-Christian tradition by scientists in the 1960s – suggesting that
it was largely responsible for 'the present environmental degradation'
because its view of nature facilitated developments in Western science
and technology[1] – were overstated, they did contain an element of
truth. And certainly, until the last ten years, there was a palpable lack

of urgency among many mainstream churches in terms of adopting a 'green' agenda. Even today, some Christians remain to be persuaded that 'the environment' is an absolutely priority issue.

The problem lies in part with the apparently different 'mandates' that the writers of Genesis see God assigning to humankind with respect to the world – one being to have 'dominion' over the created order (Gen. 1:26, reinforced by Ps. 8:6–8), the other to 'till and keep' the land in the manner of caretakers (Gen. 2:15). While the two are not necessarily incompatible – the 'caretaker' text could be said to provide the general principle, with the 'dominion' one applying within the writer's mind to the context of the dawn of time when some 'taming' or 'bringing to order' of nature would have seemed inevitable – the latter has been assumed by many influential church figures through the ages to sanction a cavalier, even playboy, attitude towards the planet.[2] While Christianity has not been the only influence on Western thought in modern times, it is not entirely blameless for the parlous state of the planet today.

What is disturbing is that the idea of humankind having free rein over the planet runs against the grain of biblical teaching about creation, as even a cursory glance at the Hebrew Scriptures reveals. For example, the 'jubilee' laws which the early Israelites perceived God had given them, explicitly excluded exploiting the land and maximising output from it, advocating instead a system with in-built protection for the soil in the form of cyclical rest-periods and safeguards to ensure the survival of small-scale farming. Land was not to be swallowed up by the few for their own gain but was to be for the benefit of all: indeed, it was not to be sold permanently, as the writer of Leviticus makes clear when he has God saying, 'it is mine and you are but aliens and my tenants' (25:23). Throughout the Psalms and other Hebrew texts there is a keen sense that the earth belongs to God and that humanity holds it only on trust, being ultimately responsible to God for how they treat it. As Jürgen Moltmann has written, it is the peace of the Sabbath which distinguishes the view of the world as 'creation' from the view of the world as 'nature'.[3]

We have further been led astray by bad theology in so far as we have been encouraged to see the 'next world' as more significant than this one. Clearly Scripture does caution us to prepare for the eternity which will follow our fleeting existence here below, but not to the extent of making that our main focus as believers in God. The idea that we should treat this world as little more than an airport terminal through which we briefly and carelessly pass on our journey to the beyond – as implied by some influential pre-millennial writings in the United States – hardly matches the general tenor of Scripture. That God sent his Son into the 'cosmos' (John 3:16) demonstrates how central it is to the divine plan of redemption, and in Scripture we also have the writer of Isaiah picturing a restoration of order and beauty on this planet (11:6–9), St Paul talking of creation groaning and waiting to be set free from its bondage (Rom. 8:19–23), and the vision in Revelation 21 of the refashioning of the present earth, a 'making of all things new' rather than the making of a new thing. The doctrine of resurrection – still at the heart of our major creeds – implies that the promised new age will be realised on earth, and arguably such a hope would have stayed central to Christian teaching had not the Church acquired a stake in the *status quo* in the fourth century and marginalised subversive expectations of a better order on earth! A recapturing of this vision of the earth being renewed and not destroyed might deepen our respect towards it at this crucial time.

If, with some honourable exceptions, churches have not been in the forefront of movements to protect the planet, at least many are on board now. Particularly significant, given their access to President Bush and heavy influence within the Republican Party, has been the 'conversion' of the mainline evangelical churches in the United States who, in February 2006, announced their commitment to 'help solve the problem of global warming'. Significantly, their statement also acknowledged that it was the poor who suffered most from this phenomenon.[4] With most churches in the UK now adopting 'environmental policies' and debating climate change at national, synod and local level, and the main ecumenical networks formed around environmental concern gaining considerably in influence, we can say that churches are rapidly becoming locked into the environmental cause. So how can we harness our influence and concern to make a real difference?

Getting informed

An obvious starting point is to get informed – though, as with trade justice, the issues are complex and those of us without science PhDs will probably have to manage with only a basic understanding of them. Most websites devoted to raising awareness about the environment explain the issues in straightforward terms, and articles in the serious daily and weekly publications are generally aimed at the 'thinking layperson'. But while we will want to grapple with the issues ourselves and make informed judgements about how to respond, what will probably persuade us to take action will be an awareness that 'most experts' believe global warming to be the big issue of our day and the passion of their appeals for immediate efforts to halt its advance.[5] This might also be reinforced by considering the possible motives of that dwindling minority of scientists and opinion-formers who claim that talk of an arctic meltdown is grossly exaggerated, particularly if they are known to have links with multinationals with a vested interest in maintaining our dependency on fossil, carbon-emitting fuels.

The most effective response we can make to the environmental crisis is along two overlapping lines: to make our own lifestyle and patterns of behaviour 'greener', and actively to support national campaigns to raise public awareness and secure political change. To take the last point first, while governments will need to take decisive action, it will be what we as ordinary citizens think and believe that will ultimately count. Nothing less than a change of hearts and minds on a grand scale will be needed, both to prompt an urgent political response and to bring about a radical change in behaviour. We can play an important part in helping to bring about the necessary change of culture, and by both applying political pressure and adopting a different lifestyle, we show the integrity of this crucial campaign. It would hardly be consistent to lobby politicians to put the environment first without doing so ourselves.

Personal lifestyle

This challenge to 'personal lifestyle' adds a dimension to campaigning on the environment that is not found in, for example, action around trade justice. No changes that we make in our habits as consumers – including buying fairly traded goods – will have any effect on the structures governing global trade, yet if enough of us make our homes, workplaces and churches more green, this can at least help to slow down the process towards climate chaos. We have the power – and the responsibility – to effect some difference ourselves. And there is no shortage of advice, from both Christian and secular sources, as to how to go about it.

Mayer Hillman's *How We Can Save the Planet*, and Ruth Valerio's *L is for Lifestyle* are two particularly challenging resources (the latter is written from a specifically Christian perspective).[6]

These authors offer a number of suggestions for a sustainable lifestyle that are already becoming widely adopted, including keeping the heating low in winter and wearing more clothes to keep warm, boiling the kettle less often, using energy-efficient light-bulbs, and recycling and composting virtually everything. Perhaps more controversially, they advocate cutting back on travel, particularly by plane – an issue we shall pick up again shortly. Clearly, in the areas of energy and water consumption, and the disposal of waste, there is significant potential for us to fulfil our responsibility as 'faithful stewards' of God's creation. This is also true in our capacity as consumers, if we seek wherever possible to buy goods which are sustainably produced, locally sourced and minimally packaged. A mantra we might adopt is 'Recycle – Reduce – Refine – Repair', embracing as it does a commitment to avoid unnecessary waste and to cut back on and be less tolerant of commodities and activities which harm the environment. Building on the success of the fair-trade campaign, we might seek to promote the concept of 'ethical consumerism', demanding that companies should develop a greater range of environmentally sound products. Such pressure can help to persuade companies that 'going green' makes good business sense in the long run.

Church lifestyle

Many of the measures we adopt to make our own homes more sustainable could also be implemented by our churches. While keeping the heating turned down on a cold winter's morning will hardly help the congregation focus on worship or make newcomers feel welcome, practices like recycling and composting, using low-energy bulbs, being careful with water, and using washable crockery and cutlery can easily be adopted in a church context. Switching to a green energy supplier is a crucially important step for a church to take, and help with this can be obtained from Christian Ecology Link (CEL), whose 'Operation Noah' project actively encourages this. Operation Noah also encourages churches to sign the 'Climate Covenant' which commits them to campaign for action by world leaders to avert climate change and to take action themselves to reduce greenhouse-gas emissions.[7]

Some churches have explored switching to solar heating, and grants are sometimes available for this. A church in Lewisham in south London, for example, installed a solar panel and a wood-fuelled heating system – resulting in enormous savings on its energy bills and a 90-tonne reduction in its fossil carbon dioxide emissions every year – following receipt of a grant from a leading energy company made possible by the Green Energy Fund scheme. From time to time governments have adopted grant-making criteria for projects aimed at changing public attitudes to tackling climate change. Churches with land might also reflect on whether it is being used in an environmentally friendly way and how far there might be scope for tree-planting or for making it more welcoming for birds and other wildlife, many of whose nesting, breeding and migratory patterns are being affected by global warming.[8]

Another initiative encouraging churches to become greener is 'Shrinking the Footprint', launched on World Environment Day 2006. Headed up by the Bishop of London, Richard Chartres, and aimed at Church of England parishes, this project invites congregations to complete a questionnaire relating to their current levels and types of energy consumption and whether, for example, they encourage car-sharing and provide space for people to leave bicycles. The information provided by this audit will enable a 'benchmark' to be established and the size of the Church of England's collective 'carbon footprint' to be assessed, followed by a series of initiatives to 'shrink' it.

Most of the mainstream British denominations have adopted 'environmental policies', which can be very useful in encouraging and resourcing local congregations to act in more sustainable ways. The following extract from the Environmental Policy for the United Reformed Church, based on that of the Methodist and Baptist churches, is fairly typical and could provide the basis for a policy for other churches as yet without one:

> In order to work out our faith and fulfil our responsibility for the stewardship of God's creation, we commit ourselves to the following actions:
>
> *Awareness and Commitment*
> - promoting awareness among our congregations of these principles and objectives and of the values underpinning them;
> - ensuring that all staff members of the United Reformed Church, its synods and colleges are familiar with this

environmental commitment and its objectives, and encouraging them to work towards its implementation;
- encouraging United Reformed Churches in their activities to comply with all relevant environmental recommendations for good practice.

Energy and Water
- ensuring energy is used efficiently and whenever possible conserving and reducing its use;
- encouraging the increased use of renewable energy, especially green electricity, and using water efficiently and with care;
- preventing pollutants from entering the drainage system.

Waste
- reducing the production of material waste including unnecessary packaging;
- encouraging the re-use, repair and re-cycling of materials including organic waste;
- disposing of waste in a safe and responsible way;
- adopting environmentally sensitive purchasing policies, for example recycled paper.

Materials and Resources
- buying products which are made in accordance with the principle of using material in a sustainable way and using locally made or produced goods and food as far as this is possible and practicable;
- buying products from sources that adhere to principles of fair trade, especially mindful of those within poorer countries;
- taking into account the lifetime costs and embodied energy of materials when repairing, altering or rebuilding premises;
- offering electronic communication as an alternative to paper for those who are suitably equipped.

Natural and Built Environment
- taking appropriate opportunities to conserve and enhance the natural and built environment;
- engaging with local planning developments where these affect the environment;

- encouraging the renewal and enhancement of the urban environment;
- being sensitive to the impact of church activities on the local environment;
- ensuring church-owned land is used in ways that will protect the environment.

Travel
- making every effort to reduce air pollution and energy consumption resulting from the use of cars and planes by avoidance of unnecessary travel and the use of energy-efficient vehicles;
- exploring undertaking the work of the denomination and local church in ways which reduce the need for travel, particularly by car and plane, and encouraging the use of public transport;
- sharing car transport whenever possible.

We affirm that the earth belongs to God and hold to a vision of a world that reflects the glory of God. So together we will celebrate all that is done and achieved in fulfilling our human responsibility for the care and stewardship of creation.

The statement also commends two projects and 'encourages their use amongst our churches as a way of living out our environmental policy'; these are Eco-Congregation, an environmental tool-kit for local churches established by the partnership of the Environmental Issues Network of Churches Together in Britain and Ireland (CTBI) and ENCAMS ('Environmental Campaigns'); and Operation Noah, an initiative of the Christian Ecology Link and CTBI which seeks to raise awareness of, and promote action around, the issue of climate change. Both projects, the statement notes, 'supply materials and assistance in raising the awareness of congregations to our stewardship of creation, for enhancing worship and Bible study, for working with children, young people and adults, and for taking action of a practical nature in our church life and within our communities.'

Challenging our communities

Churches can give a lead by example in our communities, whether in a rural, urban or suburban setting. One church in the Leicestershire countryside, for example, identified a need for a shoe-recycling facility and installed one; another, in Sussex, gave out low-energy light-bulbs at a community Candlemas service; and in inner-city Derby one church organises regular litter-picking outings to local eyesores and another runs an aluminium-recycling project. A church in Edmonton, north London, has fitted 117 solar panels to the roof of its hall to create an alternative power source, and in Tosside, Lancashire, a wind turbine capable of powering all the major facilities in the building has been installed by a church – and blessed by the local bishop! Churches can include a 'green tips' section in their newsletter; lobby their local council to introduce or improve recycling facilities and ensure that roads and town centres are more pedestrian- and cyclist-friendly; run workshops or craft clubs where unwanted goods are converted into useful or decorative items for resale; organise and publicise a 'no-car Sunday'; offer their full-time workers a cycle mileage allowance as well as a car one ... the possibilities are endless, and further information and advice can be obtained from networks such as Eco-Congregation, which inspired and resourced some of the schemes mentioned here.[9] Eco-Congregation encourages churches to carry out a 'green audit' and runs an award scheme for churches adopting green practices.

Thinking on a larger scale, churches do have the potential, in seeking to serve their local communities, to give a lead towards radically transforming them through environmental concern. Living a green lifestyle by definition impacts on our local neighbourhood, and a church could be a catalyst for developing a whole new culture which takes seriously the business of buying locally, sharing vehicles, developing community allotments and so on. Over time the impact of such activities on a local economy could be far-reaching, bringing advantages in the form of cheaper food, more efficient local transport and increased employment opportunities, to name but a few. These would also be likely to widen participation further, perhaps even fostering new models of community organisation and decision-making. There is a radical theological issue here, involving developing a resistance to a prevailing culture of materialism, consumerism and individualism, and defining ourselves less in terms of what we have or earn – what one writer has termed 'affluenza'[10] – than the quality of our life together. This is a process at the heart of the 'culture-shift' we identified earlier as vital if we are to avert disaster.

Using worship

Our worship also presents opportunities for raising awareness about the environment. Harvest festivals, Rogation-tide services and special services of thanksgiving for animals can be used to highlight our need to care for God's planet, and in the regular Eucharist, Mass or Lord's Supper the earthy origins of the bread and wine – acknowledged in some liturgies – can be underlined (together with the water, fire and other elements which are present and represent the inclusion of the whole of creation).[11] One organisation producing worship materials with an environmental focus is A Rocha, whose website offers downloadable service orders suitable for a wide range of service types together with sermon outlines, small-group materials, song and hymn suggestions and copiable visual materials. A Rocha promotes 'Environment Sunday' (formerly 'Conservation Sunday') – when churches can particularly focus on the environment – and encourages churches to explore working jointly with local Wildlife Trust groups. Through its Society, Religion and Technology (SRT) Project (one of the longest-running church initiatives on the environment), the Church of Scotland has produced a special liturgy focusing on climate change.

Sermons and talks can stress God's nature as creator and sustainer of life and challenge us to be good stewards of the world. Messages that emphasise God's presence in creation through the Spirit, and God's love for the world to the extent of sending Jesus to become incarnate among us, are helpful correctives to theologies majoring on God's 'otherness' or remoteness, which can – albeit unwittingly – engender a lack of respect for the environment. Stressing the Pauline affirmation that 'all things have come into being for Christ and through Christ' (Col. 1:16) can help develop an attitude of care and reverence towards creation.[12] There are many traditional hymns with 'creation' themes, and some composed more recently will be more explicit in their ecological focus. Some of these are often only used at harvest but could well be incorporated into worship at other times.

Getting political

Yet having said all this, making our homes, churches and communities greener will not, in the end, be enough to avert the disaster that appears to await us. This action is vital for its own sake and is a powerful way of radicalising many in our churches, but our new awareness has to lead us to engage politically, to join with those of like mind to ensure that the action that needs to be taken is taken. As with the debt issue in the 1990s, what is needed is not just a mass raising of public awareness and concern but a mass mobilisation of people around the issue such that politicians cannot avoid responding with radical action.

An important call to the churches to take the political option was made at the sixth assembly of the European Christian Environmental Network (ECEN) held in Flämslätt, Sweden in 2006. ECEN identified what it believed to be the key issues facing the planet and issued 'a call to every church and Christian in Europe' to act responsibly, raise awareness and 'engage with politicians' in this area. Operation Noah argues that, given its alliances with Europe, the USA and the Commonwealth, the UK is uniquely placed to broker a solution to the global-warming crisis. Building a strong movement among the churches to lobby the government to secure an international treaty could therefore be a way forward.

Another potentially very significant vehicle for action on climate change is Stop Climate Chaos, a network which has already attracted faith organisations like Tearfund, Christian Aid and CAFOD as well as long-standing environmental groups such as Greenpeace and WWF. The movement's key demands are:

- the UK government must deliver substantial annual reductions in UK greenhouse-gas emissions, meet its target of cutting CO_2 emissions by 20% by 2010 and commit to an EU-wide greenhouse-gas reduction target of 30% by 2020;
- the UK government must make climate change a top international priority so that global warming is capped at a temperature rise of two degrees Celsius above pre-industrial levels. This will require global emissions to have peaked and be irreversibly declining by 2015;
- the government must ensure that its policies on combating global poverty include investing in low-carbon technologies and clean energy and providing significantly more assistance to the developing world to adapt to climate change.

The involvement of churches and Christian agencies in this network significantly enhances its potential to achieve these aims; just as church people brought passion, commitment, organisational skills and sheer numbers to Jubilee 2000 and Make Poverty History, so their involvement in a similar coalition around climate change will give it extra breadth. As Operation Noah argues, there is a 'spiritual dimension to the climate crisis, which requires a contribution to be made to public debate from a faith perspective',[13] a point also made by the Bishop of London and other church leaders. The churches' involvement in Stop Climate Chaos is also evidence of the level of broad concern that exists around climate change and of the sense of urgency about the campaign. Another powerful global initiative which has enjoyed church support is the 'Earth Charter', a statement of 'common vision, values, and ethical principles for creating a sustainable future' drawn up over ten years and formally endorsed by over 2,400 organisations, including UNESCO and the World Conservation Union (IUCN).

Speaking out

A key role for Christians within movements for environmental change is to provide a 'prophetic edge', to make and support statements which are true but 'uncomfortable'. One such is that those of us living in developed countries need radically to change our lifestyle if further deterioration of the planet is to be avoided, that economic growth at current rates can only increase the damage we have already inflicted on our environment. The imperative to 'live more simply' becomes all the greater as we see the effect our behaviour has on countries in the South, where millions of people are dying and millions more are being displaced through droughts, floods and famine attributable to changes in weather patterns caused by climate change. The link between carbon emission levels in the North and the persistence of poverty in the South has been noted in reports produced by both the Department for International Development and non-governmental organisations and agencies, and as governments and politicians acknowledge this reality we must keep up the pressure for an appropriate response to be made, however sacrificial that might be in terms of our current quality of life.

Three major reports by agencies and charities – *Up in Smoke* by the Intergovernmental Panel on Climate Change (2004), Tearfund's *Dried Up, Drowned Out* (2005) and Christian Aid's *The climate of poverty: facts, fears and hope* (2006) – have asserted that the effects of climate change could be so severe as to 'nullify efforts to secure meaningful and sustainable development in poor countries' and ensure that the UN's Millennium Development Goals, which aim to halve world poverty by 2015, will fail to meet their target. Christian Aid now recommends that 'a discrete carbon-emissions goal' be added to these Goals.[14] Political parties may be increasingly convinced of the need for policies to tackle climate change and carbon emissions, but it is our responsibility to ensure that they deliver on them and that they are targeted at helping the world's poorest people. It is not a case of 'adding' an environmental dimension to our campaigning on poverty but of understanding how, if we truly cared for the planet, poor people would not suffer.

An example of the momentous decisions that we – and our politicians – need to face, is in the area of travel. Flying is now widely acknowledged to be one of the chief contributors to global warming, yet with the advent of low-cost airlines there are more planes in the air than ever before, a trend that is expected to increase. The introduction of budget fares – in some cases making the plane the most financially economical option over the train or even the coach – has greatly increased the possibility of regular flying, and in this context it is unsurprising if politicians seem reluctant to introduce measures to curb air travel and even eager to grant permission for additional runways to be built. Christians need to be among those saying things that will not be popular but which are necessary if our own and our children's futures are to be saved – and of course living consistently with them. That was what characterised the prophets of old, many of whom paid dearly for their outspokenness, and they are a powerful model for today.

Being positive

But of course we get nowhere by simply being negative: we need positive, workable proposals based on creative and informed thinking. At present the cost of flying is kept artificially low because the fuel used is not taxed, and pressure could be put on governments to make aviation pay for its full external costs, while explaining why this is necessary from an environmental angle. In its report on poverty and climate change, Christian Aid advocates a global aviation tax to be levied on airline ticket prices as a means both of curbing the runaway growth in air travel and creating revenue for development projects – adding that, in future, this tax should be transferred to aviation fuel itself.[15] Colin Challen, chair of the All-Party

Parliamentary Group on Climate Change and one of that rare breed
of politician who *has* spoken out on this issue, suggests that the
'discretionary' nature of air travel makes it unlikely that a move like
this would lead to 'fuel protests', and that it would also be an
incentive to governments to improve and make more accessible
alternative forms of transport such as rail. Challen has also floated
the idea of employers being encouraged – perhaps by financial
incentives – to allow their staff extra time off for holidays if their
destinations will take longer to reach by forms of transport other
than air. Challen notes also the economic benefits to the regions
which would be passed through instead of flown over.[16]

Another positive, workable proposal which could be embraced
and advocated more widely by churches is the 'Contraction and
Convergence' programme. This was initiated by the Global Com-
mons Institute and has been highlighted by, among others, the
Archbishop of Canterbury and the authors of the Church of England
report *Sharing God's Planet.*[17] This programme has echoes of a
'carbon rationing' scheme advocated by Hillman in his book *How
We Can Save the Planet* and, as Rowan Williams says, seeks to
achieve fairly rapid and substantial reductions in greenhouse-gas
emissions, but 'in a way that foregrounds questions of equity between
rich and poor nations'. Its core suggestion is that every person should
have the same 'entitlement to pollute' – an agreed level of carbon
emission compatible with goals for reducing and stabilising overall
atmospheric pollution – and advocates of it envisage that, since the
heavily industrialised, high-consumption nations will look to use
more than their entitlement, they will need to purchase the pollution
'credits' of less prosperous countries to the benefit of those countries.
In the medium term this should lead to 'convergence', a situation
where every citizen of the globe gradually assumes the same level of
responsibility for environmental pollution. However, since there
would be pressure on over-average users to reduce their pollution in
the long run, the 'addictive levels of dependence in wealthier countries' would be reduced and renewable energy sources would be
developed. The suggestion has also been floated that, within an
individual nation, every citizen could be given a 'personal carbon
allocation' and even a 'swipe card' to record each occasion when
points are lost through, for example, buying tickets for a flight or
purchasing petrol. Low energy users would sell their surplus points to
high users via a central 'bank'.

We will also need to produce and support constructive proposals aimed at encouraging businesses to cut back substantially on their carbon emissions. While many companies do take their responsibilities towards the environment seriously, and are of course now bound by the climate change levy introduced in 2001, a significant minority continue to contribute heavily to the rapid change in the climate we are experiencing. Data obtained by *The Guardian* under the Freedom of Information legislation revealed that, in 2005, five British-based companies alone produced more than 100 million tonnes of carbon dioxide – and that the UK allowed companies to produce significantly more tonnes of carbon dioxide than permitted under a Europe-wide scheme to tackle climate change by capping the amount of carbon emitted by the heaviest polluters. Given that these five major companies produced between them ten per cent more carbon dioxide than all of Britain's private cars put together, and that even just a one per cent increase in the efficiency of the UK's largest power station would save the typical carbon emissions of about 21,000 households, the need for tighter controls on corporate pollution to be introduced immediately is clear. Indeed, it is obvious that without them all our efforts as individuals, churches and communities will be in vain.[18] Serious political lobbying for some radical and creative approaches to cutting the volume of carbon emitted by industry has to be a vital part of our overall campaign around climate change.

Changing the culture

In the face of a culture which knows the issues around climate change and what needs to be done, but cannot make the shift to do it, we must be among those unafraid both to speak out and act, underpinning our words and actions by a lifestyle consistent with the changes we demand. This must be part of our calling as Christians. It is clear that nothing less than a wholesale mind change will pull us back from the brink of disaster, and we need to continue to be outspoken in challenging the received secular wisdom of our day. As Archbishop Rowan has put it, part of the weakness of our culture is that 'it cannot see things clearly in relation to anything other than human needs and perceptions now', nor accept that taking liberties with our planet will eventually lead to 'the palpable "revolt" of the natural order against its distortion by human will'.[19] In a similar vein, Michael Northcott calls for a recovery of the Judaeo-Christian idea

of connection between past, present and future actions and genera-
tions, such that we would include in the category of the 'neighbour
whom we are to love as our self' people who will live in the future.
Northcott mourns the way our modern lifestyle helps us to forget the
source of the energy we use – for example, the light from an electric
bulb is the physical product of the light of the sun on the prehistory
of the planet – and he challenges us to reconstitute our daily rituals,
such as flicking switches, so that we might behave more virtuously
with respect to our individual and collective use of that energy.[20]

At its heart, as Ruth Valerio has pointed out, our environmental
crisis is a spiritual issue,[21] and it is clear that a fundamental shift in
the prevailing ethos, which sees it as acceptable for people to make
lifestyle choices (for example, with respect to travel or choice of car)
without regard to the consequences of those choices – what the
Bishop of London once defined (to unjustified criticism) as 'sin' – is
vital. As Madeleine Bunting perceptively wrote: 'with a kind of
savage justice, climate change ... exposes the weakest link in the
cultural mindset of western market capitalism: the collective capacity
for self-restraint in pursuit of the common good.'[22]

Hillman has compared our own time with the Second World
War, when rationing and other constraints were accepted and a
strong sense of 'pulling together' against a common foe prevailed;
and while that comparison has its weaknesses, not least because of
the radical difference in both the nature and the imminence of the
threats involved, the experience of war does prove our capacity to
live with extreme measures when the occasion demands. Some
experts are arguing that a war-time mentality may at some point
present itself as a necessity. Since global warming is in reality a bigger
threat than terrorism, and threatens more lives, then an international
response – like that which countries such as the USA and the
UK have shown they *can* mount when they deem it necessary –
will be required. What will be vital, as the leading commentator
Andrew Simms, of the New Economics Foundation, has written, is
pressure to ensure that our leaders are not allowed to claim that they
are 'doing the best' but rather, as in war-time, implement the measures required to succeed – including, if necessary, fossil-fuel
rationing.[23]

Retaining hope

Above all, in the face of increasing fearfulness and dread, and the knowledge that things *will* get worse in the short term, we must not believe that all is lost: Christian Aid were right to sub-title their 2006 report 'facts, fears and *hope*', for the evidence shows that if we make the right changes now, we can still leave the planet in good order to our children's children's children. A massive change in culture is possible as people become aware of the reality of the situation and the part that they can play in transforming it. The process will be necessarily slow, but signs of hope can be seen in, for example, the steady increase in recycling (the national rate in the UK is now approximately 25 per cent), the growing popularity of renewable energy, and the public pressure that has led to all the major parties promoting 'green' policies. As we have noted, even in the USA, where the key to global salvation may be said to lie, change is occurring (within certain states if not at a federal level), and we should keep supporting those American churches and networks with whom we have contact as they seek to make climate change a key electoral issue and pressure politicians into radical action.

This is all so vital because, as with the linked concern of global poverty, it is with politicians that the power to make the necessary radical changes squarely lies. As we have been reminded by Ashok Sinha, who headed up the Jubilee Debt Campaign before becoming Director of Stop Climate Chaos, the 'determinant' between the two scenarios we face – unspeakable disaster on the one hand and a world in which all have access to the resources they need on the other – is 'nothing more, or less, than political will. The science is now clear that climate change is occurring ... and that the impacts could be appalling for people and planet alike. The question is whether our political leaders have the courage to take the tough choices necessary to deliver climate justice rather than chaos.'[24] What we must do is persuade politicians to act, something we have been successful at doing in the past and can be successful at doing again.

Given that climate change must of necessity be tackled on a long-term basis, we might consider supporting calls for it to be removed from the realm of 'party politics' altogether. One advantage would be that long-term strategies could be adopted which would be able to survive changes of government, another that tough and unpopular decisions could be taken by politicians without regard to the electoral consequences. Political leaders have been loath to talk about the need for policies that 'hurt', even if they believe them to be necessary, for fear of losing power to those who promise less draconian measures. Were a cross-party consensus to exist, then radical measures – even those which might impose curbs on our 'carbon-crunching lifestyles' – would become feasible. This may have echoes of the war-time 'coalition' governments of the last century, but the issue of climate change is already too serious to be made the stuff of political point-scoring or 'gesture politics'.

The full consequences of global warming are almost too horrific to contemplate. Even what the chief scientific adviser to the UK government regards as his most optimistic scenario – where the rise in carbon dioxide emissions levels off at a point that raises the world's temperature by more than three degrees centigrade – would see a further 400 million people added to those already starving or at risk from it, half of the world's nature reserves destroyed, and up to three billion people facing water shortages.[25] Other predictions suggest that sea levels will be 88 cm higher by the end of this century, resulting in 100 million people across the globe losing their homes and livelihoods. It is not difficult to picture a dystopia involving widespread hunger, drought and malnutrition, mass migration to higher ground, armed conflicts over access to water, fertile land and scarce resources, and the disappearance of numerous land-based species. And in case, God forbid, we were tempted to think this will only play out in the developing world (which will of course continue to bear the brunt of the fall-out), we need to recall the devastating and deadly events in Louisiana in 2005, the heatwaves in France which have led to thousands of premature deaths in recent years, and the fact that some four million homes in England and Wales are subject to flood risk. It ought to be impossible for people with a concern for God's creation and the well-being of our neighbour not to be passionate about this situation, not to find our hearts as well as our heads shocked by the awfulness of our planet's prognosis. Our response must be to channel our passion – and faith – into concrete action, prayer and witness.

Chapter 4

Make Poverty History
Seeing the Millennium targets reached

Let the future say of our generation that we sent forth mighty
currents of hope, and that we worked together to heal the world.
Jeffrey Sachs

World hunger is the great non-story of our day. You could read the
papers or watch the news for days and not be aware that millions of
people across the globe are facing a struggle to survive, a struggle
they will sooner or later lose. Every day 50,000 people die from
hunger or preventable diseases. If a fraction of that number were to
perish in a plane crash or a bomb outrage, the media would carry the
story for weeks. But the nameless babies, children and adults dying
prematurely every day from lack of food, clean water or accessible
health care form a kind of 'silent holocaust', brought to the world's
attention only when we deign to term their situation a 'famine' and
launch a special appeal. No British tabloid has yet invoked the nation
to a day of prayer for world hunger with the same passion as they
display when an injury to a leading soccer star looks like keeping him
out of a major tournament.

Fortunately we need not rely on the mass media for our understanding of the 'third world' (or more accurately, the 'two-thirds
world'); occasionally special reports will shock us into action, but
generally our collective consciousness about hunger, poverty and
injustice has been raised in recent years through the work of agencies,
charities and enlightened 'celebrities'. And they have brought us a
long way in our understanding: in the old days we thought that a few

pence in the Oxfam tin would do some good, and even Band Aid and Live Aid asked us to do no more than 'give our f—ing money'. Now, led by Jubilee 2000, the Trade Justice Movement and, most recently, Make Poverty History, we have come up a steep learning curve towards understanding the dynamics that keep people poor and how to lobby for lasting change. It was significant that at the 'Live8' gig in London in July 2005, Bob Geldof laboured the point that the event was not about raising money but about raising awareness and mobilising people for action. Justice, not charity, is now what it's all about.

That Christians and churches have been high profile in recent anti-poverty campaigns is hardly a cause for surprise. On one level we are disturbed, like all people of goodwill, by the evil of the situation in two thirds of the world and want passionately to see it overcome. We have no monopoly on compassion or a sense of injustice. Yet we do believe in a God who promises 'life in all its fullness', who wants all people to enjoy the fruits of his creation, and who appears on every page of Scripture as unequivocally on the side of the poor. The liberation theologians of the 1970s were right when they called us to 'praxis' on behalf of the poor, with biblical reflection as a second step. We don't need the Bible to 'tell us' to work to end poverty – the situation simply demands it. But when we do come to the Word, we certainly find added impetus for our struggle for justice, knowing that it is God's struggle too.

That our goal is *justice* needs firmly to be stressed, for only as we move beyond the idea that Christians are called simply to give – however generously – to those who are less well off will we be able to make a meaningful contribution to defeating global poverty. Giving will treat only the symptoms of a situation, not its roots: as Jim Wallis often says, fishing people out of the river is fine and something we are good at, but it's much better to go upstream to find out who is throwing them in. In some cases giving money or resources to help a relative few can even make things worse, if it enables, even as an unintended side-effect, a damaging injustice to continue unchallenged. In any case, the God of the Bible is not passionate about this kind of generosity, preferring rather systems based upon justice – and even going to the extent of laying down a model of social and economic relations which would deliberately eliminate poverty. The Jubilee, which was never put into effect in biblical times but was to inspire one of the largest mass movements of the twentieth century, was actually based on the principle of 'fresh starts' to ensure that people were not condemned to a lifetime of slavery or debt, or allowed to benefit from the misfortune of others. St Paul also seems to suggest, in his second letter to the fellowship at Corinth, that when Christians give to the poor their intent is to bring about not just relief but also greater equality (2 Cor. 8).

The vision behind Jubilee is a startling one for those who think that Christian responsibility ends with simply giving to the poor, for passages like Deuteronomy 15:1–5 suggest that God's vision was to ensure that there would be no one poor in the community to do charity to, justice having prevailed. And while recognising the difficulties of trying to apply verses from the Hebrew Scriptures directly into our present situation, I suggest we should not be satisfied with any less a vision than the elimination of poverty. Does not God demand from us, as John Reardon once tellingly put it, real change not small change? Such a thought should inspire us in our campaign to break the cycle of poverty and deprivation that locks millions into a daily struggle at the margins of life and death.

Towards 2015

And what should also inspire us is the knowledge that we are the first generation that really can 'make poverty history'. We are constantly being reminded that we live in a 'globalising' world, with the negative aspects of this often underlined, but one of the many benefits of globalisation is that it gives us the potential to act as a 'global community' to address 'global problems' – including starvation, lack of access to safe water, poor health and education, the phenomenal spread of HIV/AIDS and environmental degradation. For the first time in its history, humankind has the potential to work together to eliminate the worst excesses of poverty in our world and, even more importantly, a workable framework to make that happen. Endorsed in the year 2000 by all 189 member states of the United Nations, as well as by global institutions, businesses, non-governmental organisations, faith movements and numerous other bodies, the UN Millennium Development Goals provide a set of numerical and time-bound targets that address key elements of human development. These eight goals, to be realised by 2015 (or, in the case of the third, sooner), are:

1. Eradicate extreme poverty and hunger (840 million people are underfed).

2. Achieve universal primary education (130 million children have no school).
3. Promote gender equality and empower women (more than 430 million women aged 15–24 are illiterate).
4. Reduce child mortality (in low-income countries, one child in eleven dies before his or her fifth birthday).
5. Improve maternal health (500,000 women die each year from complications in pregnancy and childbirth).
6. Combat HIV/AIDS, malaria and other diseases (42 million adults and 5 million children are living with HIV/AIDS).
7. Ensure environmental sustainability (3 billion people have no access to sanitation).
8. Develop a Global Partnership for Development (full liberalisation of trade could lift 300 million people from poverty by 2015).

The point about these goals is that they *are* achievable. The United Nations has itself said that they are feasible, both financially and technologically, and the challenge therefore lies in building political will at both global and national levels, and setting and reordering priorities. Politicians like Gordon Brown and former International Development Secretary, Clare Short, have frequently identified 'political will' as the crucial factor attending the success or failure of the goals. They are clear that, to succeed, these goals will not require unimaginable sums of money: for example, to achieve basic schooling for every child would cost less than people in the USA spend on ice cream, and to put in place reproductive health care for all women to ensure safer childbirths would cost roughly what women in Europe and the USA currently spend on perfume. The $50 billion that the rich countries spend annually on aid to the poorest countries is tiny compared to the $350 billion they spend on agricultural subsidies. No, what it will take to see these goals realised is a change of heart by those with the power to make the big decisions, the 'political will' to make it happen. As Bob Geldof once perceptively put it, people in Africa are not dying of drought, they are dying of politics.[1]

It seems that here is a clear and direct challenge to the churches, for what will most influence 'political will' is lobbying, campaigning and raising awareness on issues of global justice, and in these activities the churches have been highly effective. It is often said that Jubilee 2000 'failed' because it did not achieve all that it set out to do by the time it set itself to do it, but such a view ignores its tremendous achievement, acknowledged by many senior politicians, in getting the issue of third-world debt into the consciousness of virtually the entire Western world and onto the agenda of the world's leaders whenever they meet. Sources close to the G8 leaders who met at Birmingham (1998), Cologne (1999) and Genoa (2001) speak of the profound effect that the Jubilee 2000 and 'Drop the Debt' rallies in those cities had, particularly because the protesters were people who would not normally engage in street action of this kind. No wonder the economic commentator Will Hutton was moved to write at what he called 'the end of an increasingly secular century' that it has been the Bible and the 'moral indignation of religion' that have challenged 'the hitherto unassailable citadels of international finance' and that it is no longer Morris, Keynes and Beveridge who inspire and change the world, but Leviticus.[2]

Where once only a small cognoscenti had any understanding of 'third-world debt' or the role it played in perpetuating poverty, now significant numbers of young and old in our society know it is an important issue. Where once world leaders could meet to discuss economic issues without confronting the question of debt, now their agenda cannot omit it. And this is without mentioning the very concrete achievements of the Jubilee campaign in terms of securing the cancellation of some $100 billion of debt world-wide – which has already led to the provision of thousands of new classrooms and clinics in countries like Uganda and Tanzania – and the commitment by the UK government to write off all monies owed to it by selected poor countries. Sustained, informed, targeted campaigning does work and has led to a massive improvement in the quality of life for literally millions of people in the developing world. We must never forget that.

Building on Jubilee 2000's success, we should campaign now for the realisation of the Millennium Development Goals by the target date of 2015. I want to suggest that this is one of the most important things that we can do as churches and individuals in our day. Clearly, of course, our campaigning should focus on specific issues and intermediate or short-term realisable targets, but this is possible through, for example, coalitions and networks like the Trade Justice Campaign, the Jubilee Debt Campaign, Stamp Out Poverty and Stop AIDS, and also by lobbying our government to increase the percentage of our Gross Domestic Product that we spend on overseas aid.

Increasing aid

To take the last point first, it has been estimated that if the UK met the internationally agreed target of 0.7 per cent of national income in aid by 2008, an extra 1.5 million people could be lifted out of poverty. What we are in fact committed to doing by 2008 is raising that percentage to 0.47 per cent, some way short of what we should be allocating and 0.04 per cent less than we were spending in 1979. Looked at in context, of course, these figures show that some progress has been made in recent years: in the six years (1997–2003) of Clare Short's tenure at the then newly created Department for International Development, the UK doubled its aid spending and has continued to increase it since. But we must push our leaders to do more and do it faster. Again, we are not talking huge sums: while the UK devotes £3.6 billion to aid, it spends some £30 billion on defence, £90 billion on health, £90 billion on education and £110 billion on social security, and those who are most informed suggest that we can afford to give more aid without reducing these other very necessary budgets.[3] We must therefore continue to press our case, for, as Professor Jeffrey Sachs, one of the world's leading experts on fighting poverty, has said, 'the effort required of the rich is so slight that to do less is to announce brazenly to a large part of the world: "You count for nothing."'[4] In God's eyes, no one counts for nothing, and we need to say so.

Given that countries such as the United States and Japan are not committed to reaching the 0.7 per cent target, we should really press our government to go beyond the 'bare minimum': there is nothing particularly magic about that figure and it is clear that extra revenue will be needed if the Millennium Development Goals are to be met. In fact world leaders frequently speak of the need for 'new money' to be found if the Millennium targets are to be achieved, the figure of $50 billion per annum being most regularly quoted. Accordingly, one campaign to which we should give serious attention is the one calling for a stamp duty to be levied on sterling currency transactions at 0.005 per cent. Promoted by Stamp Out Poverty, a coalition of more than 50 organisations including churches and Christian development agencies, its strap-line is that even such a small levy on the 160 billion US dollars of sterling that is traded every day would raise substantial annual sums with the potential to increase UK aid expenditure by £1 billion without disrupting the market. Such a levy is technically feasible (given that the market is electronic), politically possible and would generate long-term, predictable income to fund strategic areas necessary to pay for the Millennium Goals. We therefore need to work at persuading politicians that this is at least one solution to the problem they have identified of finding new money for development. France and Belgium have already passed legislation for such a levy, and the UK could follow suit without waiting for other countries by imposing the duty unilaterally on all trading in sterling wherever it takes place in the world. Gordon Brown has himself warned against allowing the Millennium Goals to 'become just another dream we once had' and of our being 'the generation that betrayed its own heart',[5] and we need to say that here is one relatively painless and simple way of helping us to keep our commitment to them.

Trade justice

We must also continue to campaign for radical change to the rules governing multilateral trade, arguably the biggest single key to eliminating poverty. The Trade Justice Movement has estimated that 'currently world trade rules rob poor countries of £1.3 billion per day – 14 times the amount they receive in aid.'[6] On a trip to Mali with Christian Aid in 2002, I saw for myself the effect these rules can have, allowing rich Western nations to subsidise their cotton farmers and in consequence flood the market and drive down prices, leaving farmers in poorer countries unable to compete with cheap foreign imports, or even to cover their costs. It was heart-wrenching to see in Mali the previous year's harvest still stacked on its pallets, marooned because it would cost more to transport it than would be generated by export income, and then to find in the markets in Bamako not a single item of Malian cloth for sale. Similar stories can be told in respect of producers of other crops across sub-Saharan Africa, all of whom are on a steady downward spiral towards destitution and death as a consequence of the current trade rules and the failure of global institutions to rewrite them in the interests of the poor. The campaign for trade justice has to be one of the most important of our time, and we need to be passionate and sacrificial in our support of it.

Drop the debt

No less do we need to keep the pressure on politicians to fulfil their promises with respect to debt cancellation. Jubilee 2000 achieved an enormous amount, as we have already noted, but still 90 per cent of the debt owed by the South to the North remains outstanding. While

AIDS rampages throughout the South and millions of adults and children remain unable to read or write, some countries in Africa, Latin America and elsewhere are forced to spend more on servicing their debt than on health care or schooling for their people. Some countries have already paid back in interest more than they received in loans many years before (and for which their present governments can hardly be held responsible) and they now find that they still owe more than they originally received.

The travesty of this situation should impel us to continue to campaign on debt – through the successor to Jubilee 2000, the Jubilee Debt Campaign – aware of the real difference that has been made to people's lives in those countries whose debt burden has been lifted. One practical way for churches to support the Jubilee Debt Campaign is to become 'Jubilee Congregations', which means that they agree to take at least one action on debt each year and receive, in return, up-to-date news of the campaign as well as worship and other resources. (The scheme also extends to schools.) As well as maintaining the pressure for debts to be cancelled, we need also to call for a new process for dealing with debts that will treat poor nations justly, prevent debt relief being used as a weapon of economic and political control, and avert a new debt crisis in the future.

Defeating HIV/AIDS

Campaigning for action on AIDS is also vital in the struggle against poverty. For some Christians this can be a less clear-cut issue than debt or aid because of an assumption that AIDS is a consequence of immoral behaviour. Even if that were the case, it would not be an argument for not wanting drugs to be available where they are needed, but of course the growth of AIDS to pandemic proportions in Africa can only be properly understood with reference to the economic circumstances that lead people into risky sexual behaviour for money, or into migrating from their homes in order to work, and to a shortage of resources for proper health care, sex education and prophylactics. AIDS creates a vicious downward spiral, leaving families without parents, schools without teachers, hospitals without nurses and businesses without a skilled workforce, all serving to weaken already unstable economies. To take one example, South Africa could face complete economic collapse by the middle of this century unless concerted action is taken to halt the spread of AIDS. Lobbying our government to follow through on Millennium Goal 6, to commit to seeing that HIV treatment is more readily available in the developing world, must be integral to our struggle to see poverty overcome.

Fair trade not free trade

One of the more unusual features of our campaign against global poverty is that some of the institutions we lobby, including the UK government, appear to be on our side: indeed, it is not unusual to hear senior government ministers actually encouraging church people to put pressure on them in order to help strengthen their own position within the Cabinet and on the world stage. MPs in other parties also make similar appeals. Whilst it is undeniable that the present government has led the world in tackling poverty and that all the main political parties in the UK are committed to an anti-poverty agenda, and this is to be welcomed, important differences with regard to the 'means' do exist between campaigners and many politicians, not least in the area of trade. While campaigners and agencies are clear that poorer countries will only 'catch up' with the richer ones if they are given the option to protect their own economies – something the industrialised nations themselves did during their own periods of growth – leaders from all the main parties advocate making trade *more* free across the board, something radically different and not obviously to the advantage of poor nations at this time. 'Free and fair trade' is an increasingly common mantra from politicians of all the main parties, yet it is actually free trade that pushes down the global price of commodities like coffee, forcing millions of small producers across the developing world to sell at below the cost of production.

Campaigners actually argue *against* a level playing field at this stage, demanding rather that politicians 'tilt the world a little bit on its axis in favour of the poor', as Bob Geldof once put it.[7] We need also to beware of those multi-nationals who pay lip-service to 'trade justice' and fair trade but in practice help to make these campaigns necessary by not treating producers fairly and ensuring world prices are kept artificially low. Similarly on debt and aid, the rhetoric from politicians can be convincing and even lull us into believing that more has been achieved than is actually the case – which makes discernment and careful attention to the information provided by reputable development agencies essential prerequisites to action.

Local church action

There is much else that churches can do to advance the struggle against poverty. Along with agencies and NGOs we can continue to raise public awareness about the situation and seek to persuade those in our churches and elsewhere who remain uncommitted to the cause. Introducing a motion at a church or district business meeting, encouraging a church to support the work of a development agency, and inviting a representative from an agency to speak or preach at a service are all ways of spreading the word. A number of programmes have been specifically designed to enable churches, parishes and dioceses to come together in solidarity with people who are poor, such as 'livesimply' sponsored by Catholic agencies CAFOD, Progressio and others. In this context we need also to think more ambitiously than hitherto. For example, many local churches, and all of our main denominations, have a 'social justice' or 'church and society' department, and many support a development agency or an overseas project – but is this not in many cases little more than an 'optional add-on'?

In many churches Christian Aid or CAFOD or Tearfund is something that a small group of particularly committed people in the church 'do', and 'social justice' issues often find themselves way down the agenda at church business meetings and hurried through, once more important business like the colour of the new manse carpets has been thoroughly deliberated upon. Perhaps the time has come to challenge our churches to prove how serious they are about wanting the evil of global poverty to be defeated, and to do more than simply allocate a few minutes at the end of meetings or a 'special Sunday' to considering these issues. How about suggesting to our churches that they devote most of the agenda at their next annual conference or assembly to discussing what they can do to tackle poverty, and only then, if there is any time left over, consider matters relating to their committee structure, building restoration projects or leadership patterns? It would not only stimulate a renewed commitment by the church taking this bold and risky step, but relay a powerful message to those outside about our priorities in a world riven by injustice and destitution.

Networking with sister churches in G8 countries to encourage them to lobby their own governments is also a task for churches here to consider. Governments in some of these countries need much more 'pushing' towards action for the world's poor than UK governments, and indigenous churches can play a significant role, with other civil society organisations, in challenging public opinion and government attitudes. The obvious case here is the United States, with whom most major denominations in the UK have strong institutional and sometimes local links, though working with sister churches in some European Union countries would also reap rewards.

Fair trade
Another important and increasingly influential way in which churches are fighting poverty and injustice is by promoting fair trade. The 'Fairtrade' mark on a product gives us, as buyers, a guarantee that the people in the developing world who have produced or grown it have had a fair deal, specifically a price that covers the cost of sustainable production and an extra premium that is invested in social or economic development projects.

In many areas church people have taken the lead in lobbying supermarkets to stock fairly traded goods and encouraging local towns and cities to achieve 'Fairtrade' status. That the UK Fairtrade sector is currently growing by 40 per cent a year is also no small credit to churches. Co-ordinated lobbying of supermarket chains has brought significant results, with the majority now stocking a range of fairly traded goods, and popular pressure on seemingly less-likely companies like Starbucks, McDonalds and even Nestlé has borne fruit. In addition to using Fairtrade goods ourselves, we can press for them to be used at church and synod events, run a Fairtrade stall on church premises, and encourage members of the congregation to get the Fairtrade habit. Astonishingly, some 18 per cent of the UK roast and ground coffee market is now certified as Fairtrade, and there are more than 1000 products available in the UK with the Fairtrade mark, including fruit, wine and cut flowers in addition to beverages, chocolate, snack bars and biscuits. Even fairly traded wedding rings will soon be widely available. Clearly, if we are able to afford to buy these products regularly, it is good news for producers in the developing world, though we should not mistake 'fair trade' for 'trade justice' and forget the need to focus on the structural reasons why poor farmers so rarely get a fair deal.

Asking difficult questions
Finally, churches should also be among those asking the difficult questions and making the problematic connections with respect to

poverty reduction. We need to be among those challenging the terms in which the debt issue is framed, asking who is really in the debt of whom, given that we in the rich North have prospered for years at the expense of the poor, thanks to the inequities of the global economic system. We need to be among those calling for joined-up thinking by governments in terms of how our treatment of the environment impacts on the lives of poor people in the developing world. Tearfund and more recently Christian Aid have spelt out how poverty and climate change are 'inextricably linked' and how it is the most vulnerable communities in the world who are suffering – and will continue to suffer – disproportionately from the effects of global warming.[8] We need to challenge the system which allows multinational companies operating in developing countries to avoid paying taxes to the governments of those countries, often by using off-shore tax havens. The huge sums lost could be used to alleviate poverty or build an infrastructure for business to develop. And we should be prepared, where we perceive their analyses or policies to be inadequate, to challenge development agencies to go deeper in exploring the causes of poverty – beyond what Wilf Wilde has identified as a 'theology of discontent' towards 'a fuller gospel that better understands today's political economy . . . [and] the extent of the powers we face', including empire and global capitalism.[9]

Perhaps most difficult of all, we need to be among those pressing our political leaders to see how futile a 'war on terrorism' is without a concomitant war on poverty and injustice. Jeffrey Sachs has spoken of the world never being safe while extreme poverty, disease, hunger and deprivation continue, Kofi Annan has referred to the impossibility of development without security and security without development, and Jim Wallis of the Sojourners Community in Washington has argued that the 'war on terrorism' will only achieve limited results while some of terror's root causes are ignored. Wallis often speaks of the need to 'drain the swamp of injustice around which the mosquitoes of terrorism breed'. Like everybody else, Sachs, Annan and Wallis know that terrorism is an extremely complex phenomenon, yet their claim that poverty and injustice must be addressed because they help to make the world increasingly unstable is palpably right.

'This stuff works . . . sometimes'

After 2005, when so much was invested in trying to convince world leaders to 'make poverty history' through action on debt, trade and aid, it was perhaps to be expected that campaigning would be less intense. Lobbying by agencies has continued apace, but poverty has dropped out of the headlines and it may be some time before we witness again mass action on the scale we saw around the Gleneagles summit. Yet the challenge for us as Christians is to keep going when the issue is no longer fashionable, fighting on because the cause is just, because we believe change to be possible and because we are determined to bring it about, how ever long it takes. Apart from our unshakeable belief in a God who sides with and vindicates the poor, we know from history that no significant change occurs overnight. All who have worked to achieve justice – William Wilberforce, Josephine Butler, Martin Luther King Jr, Nelson Mandela – had to dedicate their whole lives to the cause. Therefore we are prepared to accept that it may take decades of sustained campaigning and action before we see poverty finally overcome – while we are also aware, from our own experience, that changes we barely dared hope to see, like the ending of apartheid in South Africa or the dismantling of the Berlin Wall, can occur suddenly and peacefully.

We also have the encouragement that our campaigning and pressure does work. While initially agencies and commentators were downbeat about the outcome of the G8 summit in Scotland, reflection one year after was considerably more positive: debt relief and extra aid had begun to materialise, and tangible benefits have been apparent in many parts of Africa. *Guardian* commentator Larry Elliott noted in July 2006 that the G8 'delivered just about as much as could be expected in a world in which resources are not unlimited and there are hard political choices to be made',[10] and Paul Vallely, adviser to Bob Geldof and co-author of the Commission for Africa report, said on the first anniversary of the G8 that 'the lesson of 2005 is that all the campaigning did make a difference'. Every time a mass action took place within earshot of the world's leaders, Vallely revealed, whether in Edinburgh or Hyde Park, 'more concessions were made behind the scenes by reluctant G8 governments'.[11] Pressure since Gleneagles has resulted in further successes – for example, the World Bank being forced to cut the period it had set for implementing the G8 deal on debt from fifteen months to three. Campaigning *does* work, and we need to thank God for these gains and use them to encourage both ourselves and others to press on in faith. As Geldof himself said at the end of 2005, 'the individual is not powerless in the face of either political indifference or monstrous human tragedy ... You can change the world. And millions of you did that this year. This stuff works. Sometimes.'[12]

As well as these concrete gains, our hard work has also brought development into the mainstream. Experts talk about the increasing influence that charities and NGOs are having on issues such as trade and the environment at the global level.[13] On one level, no political party can now afford to ignore the evil of global poverty, and on another, a whole new constituency has been radicalised into action much broader than 'traditional' debt and trade campaigning. A survey for Oxfam's 'Generation Why' website found that 84 per cent of people aged 16 to 25 considered that the Make Poverty History campaign and the Live8 concert had had the biggest impact on them in 2005, ahead of London's Olympic bid and the general election. Some eight million people in the UK wore white wrist-bands that year, with half a million writing to the Prime Minister and a quarter of a million attending the march and rally in Edinburgh. Churches had no small hand in this development, an external evaluation commissioned by Make Poverty History revealing that they and faith communities generally had created an important bridge between traditional activists and younger first-time campaigners. Church and faith groups had been 'the unsung heroes' of the 2005 campaign, the report concluded.[14]

Yet much remains to be achieved. Despite increases in aid and debt relief in recent years, more money still flows out of Africa to the UK than goes the other way. Trade rules are still grossly unfair to poor countries across the globe. Debt cancellation still comes with 'strings attached' in the form of requirements to privatise services and cut public spending. More than 60 countries still need debt cancellation to be able to meet their people's basic needs. AIDS continues to ravage the continent of Africa. Millions still die of hunger – or, as Geldof would say, of politics. God forbid that we ever lose our passion to see all people know 'life in all its fullness', or our belief in our potential to influence the people with power to work for justice. Signing up to the Micah Call – produced by the 'Micah Challenge' global network of evangelical agencies and churches to highlight the link between the Millennium Goals, our faith and our readiness for action in the spirit of Micah 6:8 – would be a good way of demonstrating or renewing our commitment to the long haul:

> This is a moment in history of unique potential,
> when the stated intentions of world leaders

echo something of the mind of the Biblical prophets
and the teaching of Jesus concerning the poor,
and when we have the means to dramatically reduce poverty.

We commit ourselves, as followers of Jesus,
to work together for the holistic transformation of our
   communities,
to pursue justice, be passionate about kindness, and to walk
   humbly with God.

We call on international and national decision-makers
of both rich and poor nations, to fulfil their public promise
to achieve the Millennium Development Goals
and so halve absolute global poverty by 2015.

We call on Christians everywhere to be agents of hope
for and with the poor, and to work with others
to hold our national and global leaders accountable
in securing a more just and merciful world.[15]

Chapter 5

Make Poverty History Here
Tackling injustice nearer home

> Poverty isn't just a place in Africa. It's a street not far from where you live.
>
> Jonathan Sacks

Make Poverty History's achievement of keeping Africa in the spotlight throughout 2005 had at least one unintended consequence: it helped take our eye off the situation nearer home. So effective was the campaign in alerting us to what unfair trade rules and unpayable debt can do to people in the developing world, we almost forgot how the global economy can impact negatively on communities and individuals here in the UK. Debt, insecurity, child poverty, low wages and exploitation are not just 'third-world' phenomena but all too evident in our own society.

So the 'bias to the poor' which we find in Scripture does not have meaning only once we leave these shores. Indeed, I would argue that we need to get as passionate about defeating poverty at home as we are about tackling it overseas. In recent years church leaders, politicians and think-tanks have called for a renewed commitment to eradicate poverty in the UK – even for a mass campaign along the lines of 'Make Poverty History' – and we need to hear what they are saying.[1] There is certainly a strong theological imperative to address the situation on our own doorstep, for while 'charity begins at home' may not be a biblical expression, the model that Jesus gives us through his actions and parables is very much 'do good to those at hand'. Luke's version of Jesus' commission to the disciples includes the words 'beginning from Jerusalem' (24:47), the place where they then were. Here in the UK just as much as elsewhere, people are missing out on the 'fullness of life' that Jesus came to announce. Yet UK-focused campaigns are massively less well supported than those targeting the 'two-thirds' world, and knowledge about the situation here is much less developed and widespread. As Chief Rabbi Jonathan Sacks has put it, 'it's as if we have a kind of moral long-sightedness that allows us to see destitution in the distance quite clearly, but only vaguely if at all when it's close.'[2]

Many of us are even unclear about what 'being poor' *means* in our context, perhaps because, as Fran Beckett of the Church Urban Fund has said, we are talking here about a poverty which is 'not as in-your-face as a child with distended stomach and flies in their eyes'.[3] Poverty is often more 'hidden' here – for example, in parts of our seemingly wealthiest towns, cities and villages – than in the developing world. We also tend to believe that our advanced, developed economy has the mechanisms to 'cope' with the problem, that having a welfare state rules out any need for 'charities' with a UK focus. If there are 'poor' among us, it is because they have chosen to live that way or have brought it upon themselves, not because, as elsewhere, 'the system' keeps them poor.[4]

The ignorance that we have about poverty on our doorstep is quite alarming, as recent studies have shown: one survey conducted by the Church Urban Fund in 2006 suggested that half of us do not know where the poverty line is drawn in terms of weekly income in the UK (£100 per week for a single adult), and only one in seven know that poverty might lead to ill health and poor nutrition.[5] A Fabian Society report has noted that, while in 1994, 71 per cent of people thought there was 'quite a lot' of poverty in Britain over against 28 per cent who thought there was 'very little real poverty', by 2003 these figures were 54 per cent and 41 per cent respectively.[6] It is an irony that, as a nation, we are more informed about and geared up to tackle the poverty in the world that we have not seen for ourselves than that which we confront every day.

Clearly, one challenge for us as churches is to tell the truth about the situation – that here in Britain, despite very significant improvements in the past ten years, more than eleven million people, including three and a half million children, live in poverty as officially defined. What this means in terms of quality of life and life-chances should also be made clear – for example, that infant mortality is twice as high among children in lower social classes than in higher social classes; that a clever child from a poor home will be overtaken by less bright children from well-off homes by the age of six; and that low birth-weight babies are twice as likely to be born to mothers in the lowest social class, and thus much higher proportions in this class are born with development disadvantages such as low IQ or poor cognitive functioning.[7] Until as a nation we face these awesome and disturbing facts, and the harsh reality that people in poverty will suffer from poorer health and poorer educational opportunities than people from wealthier homes, we cannot begin to do anything about improving the situation. But tied in with this must be a concern to expose the underlying causes of poverty, for, as in the case of the global situation, we shall not be able to campaign effectively to release people from the grip of poverty unless we understand what keeps them in that grip in the first place.

We need, of course, to make sure we have our facts straight, and a good place to start is by contacting a national agency focusing on poverty in the UK. Some – such as Church Action on Poverty, the Church Urban Fund, Zacchaeus 2000 Trust (Z2K), Shaftesbury, Emmaus and Christians Against Poverty – have an explicit faith base; others – like Shelter, Oxfam, End Child Poverty and the Child Poverty Action Group – do not. A visit to any one of these organisations' websites, or a mailed request to their office for information, will bring a wealth of data about the extent and causes of poverty in the UK as well as suggested ways of getting involved in campaigns to alleviate it. Some organisations will describe the poverty they are tackling as 'relative', others as 'absolute', and this is clearly more than a semantic matter and will shape those bodies' campaigning methods and strategies. As Paul Nicolson of Z2K has put it, if being relatively poor means having 'far too little money in a very expensive developed economy', then that 'threatens survival and is also absolute poverty.'[8] But the most important thing, if we are committed to engaging with the situation, is to ensure that we have the latest information and are fully aware of the scale of the issue.

Then we need to develop a greater concern for action within our own churches. For example, a church currently supporting an overseas agency or a specific project in a developing country, but not involved in tackling poverty nearer home, might consider stretching its giving and adopting a UK-focused agency or project in addition to its overseas one. One Sunday in the year could be allocated a 'UK' focus just as special Sundays and services may be given over to raising awareness about 'third-world' issues (an ideal Sunday for this would be the nation-wide 'Poverty Action Sunday' every February). Special collections or fund-raising events could be held for Church Action on Poverty or the Church Urban Fund as well as for Christian Aid, CAFOD or Tearfund. A 'parish action team' could be set up to promote the chosen agency's work. Time could be given to reflecting on how to become a 'Just Church', in response to the programme of that name developed by a number of mainstream churches and agencies in 2007. What is required is less a set of bright new ideas than a change of mind-set. We all need an expansion of our purview to recognise that debt, homelessness and malnutrition are here in the UK as well as in Africa and Latin America, and a godly passion to see them overcome wherever they exist.

Central to our work of consciousness-raising will be a concern to tell the human stories behind the statistics. As with campaigns to tackle developing-world poverty, statistics on their own move few people to act: narratives and pictures do, and UK-focused charities have (sadly) such stories in abundance. Painting the picture of a child wanting to stay at home on school 'mufti' days because her family can't afford the latest fashions and she will be laughed at, or of a student persistently late for college because he sleeps every night in an armchair under a coat, will have far more impact than lists of facts and figures.[9] As people committed to truth-telling, we need to help break the simplistic stereotyping that goes on in some sections of the media regarding the so-called 'deserving' and 'undeserving' poor, the 'spongers' and the 'benefit-cheats', and find out and re-tell the real stories of people struggling to make ends meet.

Niall Cooper, National Co-ordinator of Church Action on Poverty, has argued that portrayals of poor families in popular TV series can reinforce 'all our worst prejudices about the great unwashed – a foul-mouthed, lazy and amoral bunch, constantly on the make'. These programmes can also serve to 'poison public attitudes, permeate policy and undermine the political will to tackle poverty.'[10] As Cooper says, we still have a culture of blaming the poor for their poverty in this country, something which is now unthinkable with respect to the developing world, and the challenge to us as Christians is to help to change that. Our core commitment must be to ensuring that people living with poverty retain their dignity – which is rooted in their being created in the image of God – and that their own experiences, attitudes and ideas about change are listened to, valued and respected. As Professor John Veit-Wilson, one of our leading experts on poverty and its causes has noted, in our 'marketised society' poverty not only means not having enough cash or disposable assets but being 'treated with a lack of respect for one's dignity because of one's poverty'.[11]

Tackling the causes

We need to underline the distinction between measures to alleviate the worst effects of poverty and action to tackle its root causes and see it abolished. Churches have always been in the forefront of efforts to improve the quality of life of the poor and marginalised in society, as those with even a cursory understanding of the work of religious orders, the Salvation Army and numerous faith-based charities and organisations will know (some of which we shall refer to later). Where they have been much more hesitant is in seeking to understand and transform the processes which keep people poor, a move which would involve direct political engagement. It is significant that a survey of attitudes to poverty in the UK conducted in 2006 found only 11 per cent of respondents believing that 'religious leaders' were doing the most to tackle it, as opposed to charities and non-governmental organisations (64 per cent) and central government (28 per cent).[12] Yet political action is vital if we are to root out that which prevents one in six of our fellow citizens from enjoying even a basic standard of living and begin to tackle the malaise in our society which has prompted initiatives like the 'Respect' agenda.

All anti-poverty organisations stress the need for sustained pressure to be put on politicians: they recognise that, just as with the struggle to defeat poverty in the southern hemisphere, it is political will that will ultimately determine whether significant change occurs. One focus for our lobbying could be the concrete commitment by Prime Minister Tony Blair in 1999 to see child poverty eradicated within 20 years. We need to acknowledge that considerable progress towards that goal has been made to date and that at the end of the first quarter (2004) the target was on course to be met, with child poverty having been cut by 800,000. But that is all the more reason for us to keep up the pressure, to ensure that complacency does not set in. Keeping up the momentum will not be easy, and the government needs to know that there is massive popular concern that they press on towards the 2019 target – of the kind that they know exists around the UN's 2015 target for halving global poverty. And this need not – indeed, should not – be a party political issue, for one of our key tasks as campaigners must be to secure an all-party consensus around the 20-year target to ensure that any personnel changes in Downing Street do not imperil progress towards it. We should challenge whatever government is in power to 'poverty proof' all their policies to ensure that they are consistent with eradicating child poverty.

Our concern for justice should also extend to the value of pensions, something entirely consistent with biblical teaching on respect for age and maturity. Advances in medical science which have increased life expectancy, and the gradual entry into the 'retirement bracket' of the post-War 'baby-boomers', mean that this will be one of the big issues of the twenty-first century, and it is one which has deeply divided politicians. Christians may have differing views on the relative merits of 'private' versus 'public' provision of pensions, but all will agree that people in the 'third age' deserve to live in dignity and that their right to do so should be guaranteed and not dependent on circum-. stances beyond their control, such as the whim of the market. The respect that a society affords its older citizens is an indication of that society's core values, and it is clear that, if politicians chose to re-order our nation's spending priorities accordingly (an issue we alluded to when discussing the renewal of Trident in Chapter 2), the state pension could be considerably higher than the present rate of around £87 per week. At the very least we should call for a full debate on the issue of pensions, which takes fully into account the question of how we value people who have contributed in whatever way to our society during their lifetime.

Other issues, too, require imaginative thinking and courageous speaking. While the boom in house prices has benefited those already owning or buying property, it has left tens of thousands of young people in urban areas and the countryside unable to afford a place to live or to get any foothold on the property ladder at all. Might we call for the introduction of measures to make purchasing property purely for investment purposes unattractive, thereby sparking a debate about whether land is essentially a commodity to be bought and sold for private gain or (as the biblical narratives of the Creation and Jubilee imply) a 'gift' of which all should enjoy a fair share.

Finally we should not lose – or allow our agencies to lose – a sense of what Catherine Howarth of 'London Citizens' and Bob Holman call 'healthy' or 'passionate' anger at the situation poor people find themselves in. Holman, who moved from a distinguished academic career as a professor of sociology to live in a poor community in Easterhouse, Glasgow, affirms that one way to retain one's sense of anger is precisely to live in deprived areas, where children under one are more likely to die than those in affluent areas and mortality rates for adults actually get worse. Holman encouraged the Blairs, upon their retirement from No. 10, also to live among people on low incomes in order to be of help to them and learn how poverty and inequality can be tackled.[13]

Narrowing the gap

Campaigning for change around poverty will not be without its risks. To be effective it will involve saying things that are unpopular and which question the 'received wisdom' of our day – just as, of course, Jesus himself did as he challenged those around him about their possessions and attitude to the poor. In the face of a tacit assumption that poverty can be reduced without materially affecting the standard of living of the better off, Christians need to be among those saying that those (including themselves) who enjoy a comfortable lifestyle do so to some extent because some in our society receive low wages. We need to be saying that abolishing poverty in effect involves 'redistributing power over resources', creating a more inclusive model of society based less on greed and individual consumption and more on community and partnership. We need to be honest about what this may mean for our tax system, which still allows the bottom fifth of workers to pay a higher proportion of their income in tax than the top fifth, and even daring to suggest that the comparative wealth many of us enjoy is, in part, a consequence of the rates of tax we pay. And we should also highlight recent independent research which indicates that narrowing the gap between rich and poor in a society produces a stronger and more stable community, one more likely to generate trust, reduce violence and crime, increase life expectancy and improve social mobility. This research, undertaken by Professor Richard Wilkinson of the University of Nottingham Medical School, provides the first real evidence that inequality is the most important explanation of why, despite their extraordinary material success, advanced societies are often social failures, and how, when income differences between rich and poor are smaller, outcomes are invariably better.[14] When few are prepared to challenge the belief that gross inequalities in income are of no consequence and that no alternative to the unfettered operation of the market can be conceived, we should be unafraid to assert that the thorny issue of inequality must be addressed by any society serious about improving radically the quality of its members' lives. Our commitment to 'the common good' will inevitably make us concerned when we see the gulf widening between rich and poor and prompt us to ask how inclusive our society is and for whose benefit it is operating.[15]

That inequality is often not discussed is due in part to a prevailing tendency to label as 'whingers' or 'envious' those who dare to comment on examples of conspicuous consumption by the better off in our society. It is not an issue that mainstream politicians seem willing to address, yet it can hardly be a cause for satisfaction that conditions in many of our cities and rural communities are little better than they were in the nineteenth century. While some city traders annually take home bonuses in the millions, and salaries of £100,000 per week are not unusual for many in 'public life', thousands of older people die every winter because they cannot afford to keep their homes warm properly and tens of thousands of families live in temporary accommodation because they cannot afford to get on the property ladder and there is a shortage of affordable rented housing. Another indication of the widening gap in our society is that, whereas in the 1980s a chief executive of a FTSE 100 company earned around 25 times the 'average' salary, in the 2000s it is close to 120 times – and it is not always clear that high salaries are rewards for wealth creation that has benefited society as a whole. Sometimes big pay-offs are essentially 'rewards for failure' which fuel further unease among ordinary workers.[16]

As churches we should be prepared to speak into this situation, highlighting both concrete measures which would enable people to move away from poverty – such as the need for more affordable housing and an independently-assessed 'living wage' – and the evidence that shows how gross inequality harms not only the poor but the cohesion and well-being of our society as a whole. Perhaps we might call for a 'maximum wage' to go with the minimum one. Better, we might raise our game on this issue and seek to stimulate a public debate around the values of generosity and giving, recognising the absence in the UK of a 'giving culture', a sense of putting something back into the community, such as one finds in the USA.

No society can legislate to make people generous, but churches can do much to highlight the moral issues involved and, through witness and example, seek to change the culture – with potentially far-reaching consequences. Encouraging wealthy individuals and institutions to be more publicly linked with poverty reduction, including through corporate social responsibility programmes, could well meet with a ready response at a time when these bodies are increasingly perceived to be 'part of the problem' on account of the high profits and bonuses that attend their activities. As the authors of *Faithful Cities* have put it, while Judaeo-Christian teaching is not against the wealthy, it does make a 'stern challenge to those who are rich but ignore the needs of the poor'.[17] The scriptures outlining the 'Jubilee' not only speak to our time with regard to debt cancellation but by enshrining the principle that communities cannot thrive when a fixed gulf is allowed to develop between rich and poor.

Tackling debt

Effective campaigning on poverty will also draw us into issues like debt and asylum. While the iniquitous debt burdens carried by many poor countries have rightly preoccupied us in recent years, less attention has been given to the debt which exists 'on our doorstep'. Recent surveys suggest that some four million people in the UK – one in fifteen of the population – are living in households burdened with debts they cannot afford to repay[18] and that it is the poorest people who are most likely to be trapped in debt and to compound their situation by borrowing from doorstep lenders – some of whom set interest rates as high as 170 per cent per annum. As Ann Pettifor – who led Jubilee 2000 during its heyday in the 1990s – has noted, despite an apparently strong global economy, insolvency, home repossessions, individual bankruptcies and other manifestations of debt are on the rise in the UK, creating a situation that demands of our church leaders that they speak out about the effects of 'usury' and a lack of ethical standards in our society in matters relating to finance.[19]

Campaigning to see extortionate lending practices outlawed and opportunities for affordable credit and sound advice extended to people in poverty ('financial inclusion') is vital, and has already met with some success in the form of a new 'Financial Inclusion Fund' introduced by the government in 2004. Organisations like Christians Against Poverty, Church Action on Poverty and Credit Action offer invaluable help, advice and support to people seemingly ensnared by debt, and making this known in our communities – most of which will almost certainly contain a number of families and individuals who would value that knowledge – is an important service we can offer. Helping to set up a 'credit union' – an ethically run financial co-operative owned and controlled by its members who all share a 'common bond' through working or living in the same area – is also an immensely valuable contribution churches can make to their communities.

Asylum

Recent policies on asylum have also contributed to poverty in the UK. As former Chief Executive of the Refugee Council, Meave Sherlock, has pointed out, 'destitution has become a tool of public policy in the case of asylum' insofar as families who have failed in their claim for asylum may now have their benefits removed and their children taken into care in the hope that they will 'change their behaviour' and return to their 'home'. The vast majority, however, do not do this and instead 'disappear', becoming effectively (as one campaign has labelled them) 'living ghosts' – homeless and entirely dependent on friends, churches and Red Cross food parcels for their survival.[20]

Many churches are in the front line of responding to this situation and lobbying hard for a policy re-think, but one vital contribution we can all make to the ongoing and sometimes heated debate about asylum is to call for all involved to be respected as people created in God's image. Too often sections of the media (and some politicians) use dehumanising labels like 'failed' or 'bogus' to describe asylum seekers, making it easier for them to be used as political footballs and the stories behind their situation to be ignored. Such media tactics play into the hands of far-right parties and contribute to very warped perceptions of the issue – as, for example, when a MORI poll in 2005 found people believing that 23 per cent of all asylum seekers in the world came to the UK, the actual figure being 2 per cent! The truth is that people arriving here seeking asylum have usually left situations of great trauma and violence, suffered much emotional, physical and financial hardship in making their journey to the UK, and encountered considerable difficulty and frustration since their arrival.[21] Seeing them subjected to yet further and more extreme hardship should inspire all of us with faith – indeed, all people of good will – to protest in the strongest terms and seek a radical change in both policy and public opinion.

The plight of people trafficked into Britain for commodified sexual services has also recently come to light. It is estimated that some 500,000 people are trafficked across Europe, Asia and Africa each year and that around 2000 young women annually enter Britain against their will to work in the sex industry. Christian organisations committed to fighting this abusive practice – like CHASTE (Churches Alert to Sex Trafficking across Europe) and 'Stop the Traffik' – are calling on the churches to raise awareness of it, lobby MPs and church leaders to get the international legal framework governing this activity tightened, support those trying to break the cycle and help women caught up in it, and continue to speak out against the global economic conditions and lack of equality for women which sustain this trade.

The situation of migrant workers, brought to public attention by the tragic deaths of 21 Chinese cockle-pickers in Morecambe Bay in February 2004, is also a major concern and one which churches can help to address: a booklet produced by the Churches' Rural Group, 'Rural Migrant Workers: Modern Slavery', offers congregations a range of possibilities including providing space for workers to meet, extending workers a welcome to join their church (or help with practising their own faith, as appropriate) and providing services such as toiletry packs. Writing to local supermarkets asking them to source produce from suppliers that guarantee workers' rights in the UK – a variation on the argument that they should stock fairly traded goods from overseas – is also a vital part of the campaign to secure justice for these workers.

A report by my colleagues at the Von Hügel Institute, commissioned by three Catholic dioceses and published in February 2007, revealed the dire conditions in which thousands of Catholic migrants who gravitate to London from around the world live and work, and the challenge this presents to congregations and clergy.[22] In an attempt to combine Christian hospitality with a recognition of the state's right to police its borders, a campaign called 'Strangers into Citizens' has been launched to press for undocumented migrants, who have worked here for four years or more, to be admitted to a two-year 'pathway to citizenship'. The campaign's inspiration was a call made by the Archbishop of Westminster, Cardinal Cormac Murphy-O'Connor, in a Mass on 1 May 2006, for an amnesty for irregular migrants who are working in the UK and do not have a criminal record.

Regenerating our communities

While supporting national campaigns is vital if we are to tackle the root causes of poverty, action by churches in their own communities can also do much to highlight the issue and effect real change. A method some churches have adopted to raise concern locally is to stage a 'poverty hearing', an event which enables local people to speak publicly about their experience of poverty and stimulate action in response to it. These hearings require much careful planning and professional advice (available from an organisation such as Church Action on Poverty) but can be very effective in alerting people to what is happening in their community, particularly if the interest of local media can be aroused. Churches are also contributing hugely to the regeneration of local areas and to the 'quality of life' of people in their parishes or immediate areas. In neighbourhoods up and down the country a wealth of initiatives by churches, faith communities and faith-based networks are transforming the lives of literally millions of people.

We have already noted that churches and religious communities have for centuries played a central role in alleviating hardship and the direct provision of education, health care and social care: the practice goes right back to biblical times when God called his people to remember the orphan, widow and stranger, and the early churches distinguished themselves as 'caring communities'. But a major difference today is the extent to which the government and its bodies and agencies are seeking to partner with churches and faith communities and to make resources available for them for local initiatives. The formation in 1992 of the Inner Cities Religious Council (since replaced by the Faith Communities' Consultative Council) as a forum to enable faith representatives and the government to 'work together on urban renewal and social exclusion' was an important signal of new official interest in the presence and potential of faith communities, as have been a number of developments since. These include the Local Government Act of 2000, which required local authorities to consult with churches and other faith communities when compiling a 'Community Strategy' to improve the social, economic and environmental well-being of their area; the 2001 National Strategy Action Plan, which set out the government's vision for neighbourhood renewal and set up local strategic partnerships on which, in many areas, faith communities have been allocated places (in some cases after a struggle); the *Good Practice Guide for Local*

Authorities issued by the Local Government Association the following year which contained advice for local authorities on how to include faith-based movements in neighbourhood renewal; the 2004 Home Office report *Working Together: Co-operation between Government and Faith Communities*; the appointment, after the general election of 2001, of John Battle MP as link-person between churches and faith groups and No. 10; and more recently the establishment of the Cohesion and Faiths Unit in the Department for Communities and Local Government's Race, Cohesion and Faiths Directorate. The White Paper *Our Towns and Cities: the Future*, published in November 2000, encapsulated government thinking when it spoke of the 'valuable resources' faith communities can command and how 'these can be especially important in deprived areas if other forms of institutional support have been eroded. Faith communities are a distinctive part of the community and voluntary sector.'

So as churches we must not underestimate the opportunities that now exist for us to make a difference in our communities. As the founder of the Faithworks Movement, Steve Chalke, wrote in 2002, 'the current political climate has opened up an opportunity like never before for the church to work in its rightful place at the heart of every local community.'[23] Books and other resources abound (some are listed below) with inspiring stories of church-based community projects, advice on assessing a community's needs and getting a project started, information on obtaining funding, guidance on how to be professional, and warnings of the pitfalls. An enormous amount of careful planning needs to be undertaken before projects are begun and the most effective will emerge from networks already established in the area and a shared sense of the community's needs. Yet no church concerned to demonstrate God's love for their neighbourhood or the power of the Gospel to transform individuals, families and communities need be without the necessary advice on how to get started or examples to inspire!

Nor should we underestimate the resources available to support our work in our communities. As Baptist minister Phil Jump has written, 'regeneration is without doubt the most significant factor affecting community life and development in Britain today', and, since church-based social-action initiatives have so often been hampered by the 'low availability of resources ... the potential and scope for churches to align themselves with local regeneration programmes is ... obvious'.[24] Regeneration initiatives arrive in local communities in many guises – including Health, Education and Employment 'Action Zones' – and in all the government has allocated some £2 billion to its urban regeneration programme. And many churches have already availed themselves of a share of this enormous resource, as evidenced by the tens of thousands of faith-based projects going on in local communities, offering everything from training for employment to support for young parents-to-be, drop-in centres to furniture recycling, refugee centres to credit unions, bereavement counselling to support for elderly people and people with disability. Para-church bodies also exist to help churches cope with the sometimes awesome and complex business of applying for funding and to try to make the opportunities open to them more widely known.

It is not difficult to see why the government should encourage churches to engage in regeneration and seek to be partners with them: their deep roots in local communities, perhaps going back a hundred years or more, the potential of their buildings to provide community services, the connections they enjoy with other local organisations and faith communities, their strong 'values base', their access to volunteers; all these make them ideal partners in local projects. In the jargon of today, churches are strong on 'social capital' – those strong, reliable connections and networks which are necessary to make things happen – and 'faithful capital', a commitment to act out our values and faith, to 'practise what we preach'.[25] And there is empirical evidence to suggest that our impact is enormous, with literally millions of hours per month being put into voluntary service by church members, the equivalent in a year of tens of thousands of full-time jobs.[26] Rather tellingly, John Battle MP, the Prime Minister's faith envoy, has said that 'if faith communities withdrew their social services provision and the state had to step in, local and central government would be bankrupt.'

Yet there are important issues around church involvement in regeneration projects. One danger is that the effective provision of various services by churches may be used by government as an excuse to opt out of providing those services through the state – with potentially disastrous consequences should a church find itself unable to continue operating in this way. (This links into the wider question of whether we believe as a society that certain services *should* be provided by the state and how far churches should remain working largely with people at the margins.) Churches need to be wary of being co-opted into government initiatives or of unwittingly working

out a government's agenda, allowing it to claim credit for its commitment both to neighbourhood renewal and to involving the community itself in the process (though churches do not have to be
simply passive recipients of money but should have a role in shaping
policy in the area of neighbourhood renewal). Then there are cases of
churches who have found the funding on offer to be too project-
driven and short-term, or tied to an expectation that the project will
become self-financing – which work with the most vulnerable people
in society never will be. Churches will also be wary of being
encouraged to concentrate so heavily on a social agenda that they
end up becoming indispensable welfare centres with no worshipping
community at their heart. And churches will not want to relinquish
their right to be critics of government policy when necessary by being
trapped in a 'rich uncle' situation: as Nick Spencer has perceptively
put it, 'what good is it ... for a church to gain a whole world of
funding and forfeit its soul in the process?'[27]

Churches have been frustrated that too often funding bodies look for
quantitative rather than qualitative outcomes, that their lack of trust in
the experience and expertise of community-based and faith-based
organisations prevents them committing to long-term funding, and
that too often grants are paid in arrears, causing severe cash-flow
problems for small voluntary organisations. As Bishop James Jones
has said, while people in local communities prefer organic language like
'seeds, planting and renewal', those who control the money tend to use
mechanical language such as 'triggers, buttons, levers and targets'.[28] As
we have noted elsewhere, some authorities are simply ignorant of what
faith groups are and do and refuse them funding on the basis of prejudice or an unwillingness to believe them to be motivated by anything
other than a desire to proselytise. And some churches have found that
promises that they would have a say in how their projects would
operate and how their neighbourhood was run were not kept and thus
they achieved very little. It is certainly a different era from the days
when churches had to raise the revenue they needed for projects
themselves and in that sense fully 'owned' those projects.

At the end of the proverbial day each local church or ecumenical
partnership will decide how best to respond to the challenge to
engage in neighbourhood renewal and whether or not to seek
external funding. Yet it does have to be said that if every church were
to develop and pursue a vision for transforming their community, the
consequences   locally,   regionally   and   nationally   would   be

revolutionary. Even a cursory glance at a handful of the projects which churches are engaged in can inspire us to catch a wider vision and see the potential we have to change lives and communities:

- In Drumchapel on the outskirts of Glasgow churches have set up a drop-in centre for mothers and their pre-school children.
- Bramley Baptist Church in Leeds converted its Sunday School building into a playgroup which became the seeds of a major SureStart centre.
- Ryde Baptist Church on the Isle of Wight has converted its premises into a community centre with a café, meeting space, laundry and crèche; it also houses a SureStart centre.
- Churches in Hull have fitted out a bus to operate as a drop-in centre for women working in prostitution.
- United Reformed, Anglican and Catholic churches in Newport have set up a credit union to offer local people an alternative to 'loan sharks'.
- West Croydon Baptist Church – a short walk from the Home Office's main immigration department, Lunar House – is home to a refugee day centre.
- Christ Church Methodist/URC in East Dulwich, south London, set up a project called 'Bread of Life' to help develop a sense of community in the neighbourhood and opened a café, shop and Fairtrade centre on its premises.
- Following redevelopment, Sheerness United Reformed Church in Kent incorporated the local Citizens Advice Bureau, a youth drop-in, a '1stByte' computer training suite, a drug advice centre and a community café staffed by people with learning difficulties.
- Christians in Sheffield have converted a pub in a deprived area into a centre to help children on the margins of mainstream education.
- A large Pentecostal church in Brixton, south London, sends out 'street pastors' to work with marginalised young people and has seen their efforts contribute to a significant drop in street crime in their area.
- In Preston a Roman Catholic church and an Anglican church are jointly running family support and advocacy and befriending services to help people who are struggling socially and financially.
- The United Reformed Church in Newquay has joined with a

local Anglican church to run a soup kitchen and, with a New
Frontiers church and an Elim church, runs the only drop-in for
young people in what is the UK's most popular holiday resort
for the young.

These examples could be multiplied ten thousand times, and we
could also factor in denominationally run initiatives to enable
churches to work with their local communities, like the United
Reformed Church's 'Church Related Community Work' programme; but all are about adding to the quality of life of a community and, perhaps most importantly, working with people towards
their greater empowerment and the development of their own vision
for their community.

Complementing the work of churches on the ground are initiatives
like 'Soul in the City', which bring teams of young people into urban
areas for a week at a time to engage in activities like cleaning graffiti
from shopping centres, reclaiming parkland from rubbish and
painting community buildings. Such projects not only leave a legacy
of physical improvement in a community – for example, it was
claimed after 'Soul in the City' hit Manchester in 2000 that petty
crime dropped and relations between local police, businesses, resi-
dents and churches significantly improved – they also have an
evangelistic dimension in that local people are invited to services,
concerts and other events in the evenings. Importantly, 'Soul in the
City' also claims to provide a life-changing experience for the young
people involved. An ambitious year-long, nation-wide project based
on the 'Soul in the City' principle, 'Hope 2008', is planned for that
year. Critics sometimes dismiss such projects as 'painting railings for
Jesus' but they can be a powerful means of bringing the church to the
attention of people who might otherwise see it as irrelevant, as well as
transforming lives on many different levels.

Going deeper

As people who are concerned that all should have the 'abundant life'
that God intends, our faith will challenge us to address, not just
material hardship, but those more subtle and hidden expressions of
poverty which will often lie behind it – those which relate, for
example, to the quality of the relationships people experience and
their sense of identity and self-worth. As Tim Lawrence has pointed
out in a booklet produced by the Shaftesbury Society, material

poverty is usually only the tip of an iceberg that hides what he calls the 'relational face of poverty' – that is, poverty in terms of broken, unhealthy, oppressive and perhaps even violent relationships – and the 'identity face', which deceives us about our value, worth, ability and experience. For Lawrence, responding to poverty must involve addressing all three 'faces' of poverty and doing so from the bottom up, empowering people to create the change they want to see. Lawrence argues that the way that relationships are rebuilt and self-worth is regained is as important as achieving those goals themselves.

Guided by biblical pictures of a 'flourishing community', Shaftesbury's model of 'community development' goes deeper than those models which focus primarily on the 'economic' and suggest that 'the more we earn and consume the more developed we are'. As their booklet points out, winning the lottery does not necessarily improve the quality of a family's relationships, nor does simply having a doctor's surgery in a community directly decrease the number of people who get ill. But 'a combination of food, exercise, self-esteem and work related activities might be effective in improving people's health', and therefore we need to work with a model of development which addresses all spheres of life equally – the cultural, environmental, social, physical and educational as well as the economic and political.[29] The research of Professor Richard Layard and others is also helpful here, showing as it does that money is only one factor contributing to 'well-being' and that 'family upbringing and relationships', 'levels of interpersonal trust and community participation', 'work' and 'religiosity' matter just as much. The research does not suggest that money has no bearing on life satisfaction but that 'the size of the positive effect of income is small compared to other factors such as marriage, divorce and unemployment.'[30] A focus on this broader agenda will enable us, as churches, to make the Gospel impact on our communities more fully and help bring real and lasting change to the individuals, families and communities we serve.

Perhaps underlying our involvement will be a concern to demonstrate, against the grain of much contemporary thinking, that people are more than 'consumers' and have an intrinsic value to God, to others and to themselves. While of course we will be committed to improving the material conditions in which people live, we will also seek to serve our communities through ways that enhance the quality of the lives of the people who live in them. At a time when 'the market' seems all-pervasive, we can emphasise the importance of relationships and human interaction, of the 'quality' rather than, as it were, the 'quantity' of life. In this respect the campaign to 'keep Sunday special' is important, since, as Ann Pettifor has perceptively noted, the loss of one day in the week in which we could refrain from consuming and exploiting the land and each other signalled very strongly 'the transformation of our societies and economies from "people-centred" towards "money-centred".' Now, as Pettifor points out with only a little hyperbole, churches, temples and mosques are the only places left where money has not taken hold and where it is still possible to talk about the poor and the marginalised.[31] I suggest that, as Jesus himself challenged the received wisdom of his day concerning wealth, status and position, we have a Gospel to share which affirms human values over the purely monetary.

Social enterprise

The growth of the social enterprise agenda has created further opportunities for churches and faith-based networks to get involved in serving communities. Social enterprise moves beyond a straight-forward model of 'service provision' by harnessing the best practices of business to social action. Social enterprises are effectively businesses with primarily social objectives, whose surpluses are reinvested for social purposes in the business or the community. One of the earliest social enterprise projects was SCA Health and Social Care which, without any government grants, built up within 15 years a £7 million social business providing community transport, 'hospital-at-home', consultancy and training for local authorities and the voluntary sector, and even NHS dental practices in areas of social exclusion. A more explicitly faith-based social enterprise, Wigan-based Chrysalis Holidays, which offers respite care and educational breaks for adults with learning disabilities, was able to secure a hotel-style centre on the strength of a loan from a local Methodist Church. This proved a mutually beneficial arrangement, for while the church's money enabled Chrysalis to lever in a further substantial loan from an ethical savings bank and grow to become the most popular provider of affordable holidays for disabled people in the north, the church shared in the increase in the value of the centre's net worth, using this to develop new initiatives.

Another pioneering church-based social enterprise is Bromley by Bow Church Centre in east London. The brainchild of United Reformed Church minister Andrew Mawson, this offers a variety of health, education, arts and other facilities, employs 150 staff and has a turnover of £2 million per annum. Mawson and his URC colleague Peter Southcombe have also established an agency called 'One Church, 100 Uses', to enable under- or inefficiently-used church buildings to be redeveloped and then run as social enterprises by the local congregation or an agency. Social enterprises range from small credit unions, to projects training prisoners to set up businesses when they are freed, to a network of schools offering vocational curricula and work experience to young people most at risk of unemployment, poverty and truancy. As Francis Davis, Chair of SCA Health and Social Care and a leading advocate of this new model, has said, social enterprise encourages us not to 'look back comfortably on the tired welfare models of the past' but to 'step out in courage with a new and responsive vision of the future'.[32] It also, of course, enables churches to exercise more control over their funding.

Looking ahead

There is now a broad political consensus that church engagement in regeneration is to be encouraged and supported: as Steve Chalke has put it, 'after so many years of tension, with the Conservatives seeing charities as a substitute for government welfare provision and Labour basically seeing them as a threat to it, this new interest in genuine partnership is welcome news.'[33] Both parties in fact want to see the role of churches in welfare provision expand still further, inspired by what they have seen happening in, for example, Sydney, Australia, where the diocesan welfare arm, 'Anglicare', has taken on an enormous range of services previously provided by the state. The potential for local churches to be involved in 'building community' thus seems likely to increase, as does, too, the scope for churches to work with national campaigns addressing poverty and injustice. Calls for a broad coalition to tackle poverty in the UK, involving churches and agencies as well as the public and private sectors, are already seeing a response, and as we build up to the Olympic Games in London in 2012, churches have come together in a partnership called 'More Than Gold' to meet the challenge of ensuring that the Games' legacy is one of lasting benefit to the people and communities directly affected. It is imperative that, as churches, we stay at the heart of the struggle to see justice prevail in our own society as well as continuing to 'make poverty history' across the globe.

Chapter 6

Faith and Fear
Building bridges, making friends

> Co-existence and dialogue between nations, races and faiths is
> not just a vision – it is a practical goal. It remains the true
> beacon for humanity.
>
> Bianca Jagger

The advent of e-mail, the Internet, 'chat rooms', mobile phones and
cable and satellite TV has brought us more means for communicating
than ever before, yet they actually encourage us to engage with a
smaller rather than larger circle of people. As the Chief Rabbi,
Jonathan Sacks, has said, we now engage in 'narrowcasting' rather
than 'broadcasting'. There was a time, Sacks writes, when 'people of
different views were forced to share an arena and thus meet and
reason with their opponents. Today we can target those who agree
with us and screen out the voices of dissent.'[1]

The importance of 'meeting and reasoning' – of 'dialogue' – cannot
be overstated. A theme in this book has been the need to get to the
root of issues, to tackle the causes of injustice and conflict rather than
just the symptoms, and dialogue is a key component of this process.
Dialogue involves bringing together opposing or differing parties to
listen to each other in a spirit of openness and mutual respect. It asks
us to acknowledge and understand other perspectives and search for
common ground as a basis for moving forward. Dialogue is a way of
bridging divides, of relating to 'the other', even of healing wounds
and restoring justice when accompanied by repentance and repara-
tion. Sacks has rightly said that conversation is 'the greatest single

antidote to violence',[2] and Churchill's advocacy of 'jaw, jaw' over 'war, war', though rather clichéd now, still conveys an essential truth. We noted in an earlier chapter how effectively Christians have used dialogue to foster peace in war-torn regions of the world, and there are situations nearer to home in need of the same approach. Building trust, finding a common language, wrestling with underlying issues – these are all hard work requiring patience, perseverance, maturity and a belief that there is 'that of God' in all people. Churches therefore should be among those promoting and encouraging dialogue today. Jesus himself used conversation as a way of defusing tense situations or bringing truth to light, rejecting always retribution and 'an eye for an eye', and as his followers we should seek also to pursue this path. Indeed, I would argue that creating space for people to reason, debate and discuss is a profoundly valuable contribution that we can offer to situations characterised by tension, discord and suspicion where an aggressive, hostile or violent response is often the default position. In the face of cynicism or despair about these situations, we must believe in the possibility of healing and transformation through the peaceful and constructive medium of dialogue.

Bridge-building with other faiths

One of the most important conversations we need today, and one which Christians can play a vital part in developing and maintaining, is that between our different faith communities. In a way which we could never have predicted a generation ago, religious belief now plays a major part in shaping our culture. Our religious communities are now larger, more diverse and more in the public eye than hitherto, presenting us with both a cause for celebration and the challenge of finding ways of existing peacefully and equitably in the same 'shared space'. The speed and force with which the profile of, in particular, Islam has risen in recent years has caught many of our legislators and opinion-formers off guard, and a widespread lack of understanding about its core beliefs and traditions has not only hindered integration by Muslims into British society but has even led, in some quarters, to extreme prejudice and hostility towards them and their faith. I want to suggest that, as people who understand what it is to have a faith, and who are called both to love our neighbour and to welcome the 'stranger', we can play a vital role in promoting 'conversation' between religious communities and building bridges where divisions exist.

In this we move beyond mere 'tolerance' – a word often used to describe how indigenous people should treat those more recently arrived on their shores – to 'hospitality', a much stronger biblical concept which encompasses celebrating the presence of people from different traditions and backgrounds and building relationships with them. As the *Faithful Cities* report puts it, 'tolerance is the response of the powerful to the less powerful' and 'carries no imperative to actively help those who are vulnerable'; hospitality, on the other hand, 'calls us to enter into a relationship with those who are different' and open ourselves, in the process, to the possibility of change occurring in our own life and understanding.[3]

The need for reaching out to people of other faiths is even more acute as we struggle to respond to the issues arising from 9/11, the 7 July bombings and other 'terrorist' incidents in the UK and around the world. Following those events, and the invasion of Iraq and the so-called 'war on terror', the effects of a lack of a real spirit of understanding have been very starkly seen here (as elsewhere), with sections of the Muslim community feeling increasingly alienated from mainstream society and their religion subjected to misrepresentation, suspicion and, at times, ridicule. Churches can play a vital role in helping to repair this situation by facilitating genuine relationship-building within local areas and working to break down the prejudices and stereotypes which are so harmful and threatening to peace and good order in our society.

To be specific, there are two important things we can do that would make a significant difference: promote a better understanding among opinion-formers – and indeed wider society – of the true nature of religious belief and those who practise it in our society; and help to reverse the process of isolation felt by Muslim and other religious communities through bridge-building involving dialogue and communal action. It is not that Muslims themselves cannot do this – they have many articulate and powerful voices well able to make their case – but our support can be a valued expression of solidarity as well as demonstrating that ignorance about religion impacts on *all* faith traditions. It is also the case that some of the least balanced writing about Muslims comes from the pens of people who operate within a Christian world-view.

Challenging the language

We have noted already the ease with which some journalists and politicians juxtapose terms like 'fundamentalist', 'fanatic' and 'extremist' (and even on occasions 'fascist') with 'Islamic' or 'Muslim'. Regular listeners to certain news programmes might almost be forgiven for thinking that 'Muslimfundamentalist' was in fact one word. This coupling of terms is done so often today that it has become almost an automatic, unthinking process, with the consequence that conceiving of Islam as other than a violent creed, bent on world domination through force and terror, is becoming increasingly difficult. To begin to appreciate how this feels, we might imagine the Western media routinely labelling politicians who define themselves as Christian yet use military means to achieve their ends as 'Christian extremists' or 'Christian fanatics'. There was a faint echo of this during the US elections of 2004 when 'Christianity' became almost exclusively defined by reference to opinions held on abortion, stem-cell research and 'gay marriage'. We need to join with all believers in resisting the tendency of secular opinion-formers to 'define' our faith for us!

Aside from the disrespect shown to Muslims by labelling them in this way, the terminology is all wrong. 'Fundamentalism' is essentially a term used within Christianity to describe those who take a literalist approach to the Scriptures – which all Muslims do towards their holy book, the Qur'an. Clearly, then, a more nuanced grammar is needed for this discourse, and one challenge for us is to promote it – perhaps, as suggested in an earlier chapter, drawing more on the concept of 'orthodoxy'. Even if only out of respect for the majority of Muslims who practise their faith peaceably and in accordance with its true tenets, we should challenge the insidious demonising of Islam, with its potential both to heighten social tension and play on the fears of the 'indigenous' community. Of course, fear of 'the other' has been a characteristic of sections of post-war British society since the first incomers from the Caribbean arrived in the 1940s, but it is even more deeply ingrained with respect to migrants from the Indian subcontinent due to the added factors of an unfamiliar religion and an unshared language. Challenging popular misperceptions of Islam by promoting a better understanding of mainstream Muslim beliefs and culture would thus be an important way of breaking down this fear and ignorance which can all too easily generate prejudice and hatred.

Breaking down fear

The extent of our collective ignorance of Islam is borne out in some recent surveys. For example, a *YouGov* poll of 1800 respondents conducted the day after the 7 July 2005 bombings found that some 46 per cent of British people believed that Islam itself – not just 'fundamentalist Islamic groups' – posed a threat to Western liberal democracy. This figure had risen by 14 per cent since September 2001. Ten per cent of those polled even believed that 'a large proportion of British Muslims feel no loyalty at all to this country and are prepared to condone or even carry out acts of terrorism.' A survey by the same organisation in September 2006 found that one in six Londoners admitted moving seats on the bus or tube to get away from a passenger they believed to be Muslim, and more than one in three to feeling 'nervous or uncomfortable while travelling near a person of Asian or north African appearance'.[4]

The most effective action to combat this will be undertaken at the grassroots. National debates about the relative merits of multiculturalism and assimilation and how we can achieve 'cohesion and integration' are vital, and government, the media and national agencies are right to stimulate and encourage them. Bodies like the Faith Communities' Consultative Council (which replaced The Inner Cities Religious Council in 2005), which is chaired by a government minister and enables representatives from nine religious traditions in Britain to work together on urban renewal and social inclusion, and the much newer Christian–Muslim Forum, have important practical and symbolic roles. But the real challenge for many of us, as Leslie Griffiths has powerfully argued, is at the level of getting alongside one another, taking the trouble to get to know each other, forming relationships with one another and even allowing 'the reshaping of our intellectual, psychological, physical and emotional landscape'.[5] There is still much basic work to be done in terms simply of overcoming a lack of understanding about the different faith traditions in our communities, and in many areas churches can play a highly important role in building (or strengthening) bridges and seeking to develop communities built on trust and friendship rather than apprehension and distancing. In areas where Christians are in a minority and feeling beleaguered, this will be more difficult, but it is still worthwhile looking for ways to 'make connections'.

Given the extent to which ignorance feeds fear, simply making known to those whom we are able to reach some basic truths about

Islam and the majority of its adherents may help to break down the prejudice and stereotyping that has had such damaging consequences for Muslims in this country and the stability of our society. Even if our knowledge is very limited there are many good resources available to help us to learn about and understand better the different faiths in our community, including the resource pack (containing CDs and booklets) *The Life We Share* (published jointly by USPG and the Methodist Church) and *Faith meeting Faith: Ways forward in inter-faith relations*, also produced by the Methodist Church.

A key task has to be to try to reverse the current tendency of the media to portray more negative than positive images of Islam. For example, while we can regularly read quotes from Muslims implying that support for violence or revolution is widely held in their communities, and such quotes are of course 'newsworthy', can we not challenge the 'popular' media to give equal prominence to the fact that the vast majority of mosques will not tolerate militant preaching, that Muslim leaders have consistently condemned the London underground bombings, even that Islam expressly forbids hating anyone?[6] If the media highlighted these simple truths as often as they overtly or implicitly link Islam with militancy, revenge and murder, a significant change in our culture might be achieved. With specific reference to the events of 7/7, how often have the media pointed out that the 'traditional' form of Islam under which three of the four men who perpetrated this unspeakable deed grew up rejects military *jihad* and could never have led them to follow Osama bin Laden, or that the police report on the incident found no evidence linking these men to al-Qaeda or any other known terrorist organisation? Making such information available might help in some way to break down the widespread tendency to think of Islam as a single, uniform, monolithic – and irredeemably violent – belief system.[7]

Contributing letters or articles to the local and national press, engaging in acts of witness and solidarity with Muslims, and facilitating opportunities for Muslims to speak or write publicly about their faith and culture (perhaps in dialogue with Christians) are ways in which we might help a different picture to emerge. And we can draw upon a number of good examples. One was a public event organised in 2005 by 'Building Bridges Pendle', an inter-faith community project in Lancashire, which provided local Muslims with an opportunity to share their reactions to the events of 7 July in London. This consultation also involved Pendle Pakistan Welfare Association and other community bodies, and enabled those present – including a good number of young people – to debate issues with a panel of key community figures who had both a local and a national profile.

Another scheme launched by Building Bridges Pendle involved 'twinning' local churches and mosques, with the leaders of each place of worship pledging to work together for a year 'to bridge a common understanding' between their respective congregations and 'build a relationship of friendship and respect'. Under this scheme each congregation hosted in their place of worship a community event with their 'twin' faith building, usually including a meal. Considerable effort and sensitivity on all sides is needed to put such events together, but they have been times of genuine sharing and interaction to the extent that members of the different communities have set up their own groups around shared interests outside of the formal 'twinning' structure. A similar project has been initiated by Forum of Faiths Kensington and Chelsea enabling women of all the faiths linked to the Forum to meet and talk together.

Other examples of churches consciously making space for genuine conversation with other faiths can be cited. The St Philip's Centre in Leicester – an adapted church building opposite a gleaming new mosque – creates opportunities for regular dialogue between Muslims, Christians and people of other faiths and runs courses examining the religious and cultural questions raised by living in a diverse urban society. In London the St Ethelburga's Centre for Reconciliation and Peace, symbolically housed in a church destroyed by an IRA bomb in 1993, provides a space – which the Bishop of London has described as 'mutual' not 'neutral' – where people from all faiths can meet to dialogue with each other and critically explore the relationship between faith and conflict. It now also has a Bedouin tent outside the main church building, designed to be a place of meeting and reconciliation. Yet even in towns or areas where no formal pattern of dialogue or 'partnering' scheme exists, individual churches can welcome people of other faiths to attend their services and join in their festivals, something which has been actively encouraged by the Archbishop of Canterbury, other Anglican bishops and the Christian–Muslim Forum among others. Some Christians also visit the buildings of other religions at worship times, and the idea that Christians and Muslims should pray together is gaining ground (a survey conducted by *The Tablet* in 2006 discovered that two in three Catholics believed this to be a good thing).[8] Actions such as these can have a powerful healing effect on communities characterised by religious tension.

Such activity is not to be confused with shared worship, which, because it needs to respect the integrity of each faith, can be difficult to put together. As Sally Thomas, a United Reformed Church minister active in inter-faith work in the North-West has commented, there is always a risk with such worship 'of tending towards the lowest common denominator, which conflicts with honest dialogue that wants to disagree with the faith position of another while remaining friends.'[9] Both the Churches Commission on Inter Faith Relations and the URC Interfaith Relations Committee have recommended that shared worship is only appropriate at significant occasions such as Holocaust Memorial Day, key anniversaries or in response to specific local, national and international situations.

Many inter-faith groups and councils of faiths also help to raise awareness about the faiths in their region by setting up resource centres, organising discussion meetings around themes of shared interest such as spirituality, worship, social action and prayer, and running education projects in local schools. The latter can include helping to deliver PSHE/Citizenship programmes and offering extra-curricular projects around nationally co-ordinated campaigns such as One World Week. One inter-faith group in the north of England invited primary school children to make promises related to helping to create a peaceful community – and then carry them through – and also encouraged them to devise fund-raising projects for a school in the earthquake-hit region of Kashmir. On another occasion the group organised a poetry-writing competition. Action of this kind can have very important long-term implications, and also lead to simple changes taking place straight away, such as encouraging children not to 'segregate' themselves in their classrooms but sit next to people of a different ethnic or religious background. Another resource aimed at encouraging teenagers to discuss relations between Christianity and Islam is 'Peacemakers'. Produced by Christian agency Feed the Minds, this uses music videos and short films to 'redress misperceptions of Islam' and promote dialogue.

Showing solidarity

In the spirit of the 'good' Samaritan, acts of solidarity with communities of a different faith and culture can be especially powerful when those communities come under real or imagined threat due to events over which they have no control. Following 9/11, for example, churches in one south London borough organised their members to form rings of protection around local mosques to enable Muslims to attend Friday prayers safe from attack by people stirred up by right-wing political groups. Once it became known that three of the 7/7 bombers were from Leeds 11, local Christians worked closely with Muslims, building on relationships which had already been forged through 'Faith Together in Leeds 11', a social project involving Anglicans, Methodists and Muslims. In several areas peace marches were organised a day or two after the bombings, attracting large numbers of people from all faiths despite the inevitable short notice involved.

In some areas where far-right parties have made a strong showing in local or national elections, church leaders have come together to sign leaflets, for delivery by all the mainstream parties, pointing out the threat to good community relations posed by these parties and encouraging people not to vote for them. The defeat in 1994 of the British National Party's first local councillor less than a year after he was first elected was due, according to Ken Leech, to 'an alliance of the Christian churches, the Samuda Women's Centre, the Bengali Action Group and the trades unions' in the area where the councillor stood, the Isle of Dogs.[10] The Inter Faith Network has produced guidelines suggesting how faiths can show solidarity with one another when any faith or faith building is under attack. Called 'Looking after one another: the safety and security of our faith communities', its first section is headed 'Respond jointly – an attack on one is an attack on all'.[11]

In February 2006 the Hampshire Three Faiths Forum – a body committed to facilitating dialogue between the Abrahamic faiths – convened a meeting of leaders and members of the Jewish, Christian and Muslim communities in the wake of the publication of cartoons ridiculing Islam in some European newspapers. (Response to these cartoons had, in some parts of the world, been extremely violent and retaliatory.) The meeting involved sharing messages of peace and reconciliation from the Qur'an, the Hebrew Scriptures and the Christian Gospels, opportunities to reflect upon the message of peace at the heart of the faiths represented, and contributions highlighting factors uniting those faiths. One participant demonstrated the effectiveness of such a gathering by noting that it was 'all about making friendships and learning from each other' and that once you have done that, 'you will naturally be careful not to insult or offend each other.'[12]

It is perhaps more than coincidence that areas where good relations between different faith communities have been built up through inter-faith work have, in recent years, avoided the kind of violent scenes witnessed in places where this work has not been so prominent.

While events in recent years have made reaching out the hand of friendship to Muslims a priority, we must not forget that anti-Semitism is still at large in our society. As an All-Party Parliamentary Inquiry into Anti-Semitism in 2006 observed, the number of physical attacks on Jews in the UK has risen steadily this century, the figures for 2004 and 2005 being the highest since records began. Disturbingly, many of these attacks take place on children walking to school or synagogue, some of which are now increasing their security. The Inquiry also noted the prevalence of 'anti-Semitic discourse' as well as physical expressions of hatred. Given that hostility to Jews can be found among sections of the Islamic community as well as among Christians, the value of inter-faith dialogue as a way of combating anti-Semitism cannot be over-estimated. The work of the Council of Christians and Jews, founded in 1942 and committed to bringing together members of those two faiths, has proved immensely valuable.

Hindus in Britain, too, have expressed concerns about the extent of hate-crime perpetrated against their community, which they believe to be increasing, and a lack of response to it. In 1993, for example, 21 Hindu temples were attacked and many were burnt down, yet no one has yet been arrested or convicted in connection with these incidents. Hindus also claim that they are under-represented on public bodies and often excluded from formal decision-making structures at both local and national level, suggesting opportunities for churches to use what openings they have to seek a fairer deal for their Hindu neighbours and show solidarity with them in other practical ways.[13]

A proper framework

Bridge-building between communities is most effectively undertaken through inter-faith councils, which in many areas are now both well established and well respected. Details of such councils can be obtained from the Inter Faith Network or a guide it produces, *Inter Faith Organisations in the UK: a Directory*. In looking to engage with people of other faiths, contact with such a council, or with Christians already involved with it, will be a sensible first move. It is worth noting that inter-faith councils tend to be quite formal in structure, with set levels of representation for each faith, while inter-faith groups will be less formal and probably open to all. Where an inter-faith council does not exist, however, seeking to convene one could be an exciting and potentially important step, and an excellent resource for getting started is *The Local Inter Faith Guide* published in 2005 by the Inter Faith Network and the (now defunct) Inner Cities Religious Council (ICRC) of the Office of the Deputy Prime Minister. Most denominations are now encouraging their regions and dioceses to have inter-faith advisers, and their advice will also be invaluable throughout the whole process.

When seeking to create a structure for inter-faith dialogue and action locally, basic questions like the type of initiative to be pursued, the aims to be fulfilled and the geographical area to be covered should be considered before initial contact with people of other faiths is attempted. When deciding whom to contact, it is important to bear in mind that, like Christianity, other traditions are not monolithic (some are almost as diverse as Christianity!) and it is not always the case that a faith can be appropriately represented by just one person. A check on the internet or with a reliable reference work will help to ensure that all the different groups and denominations within each tradition have been included.

One should not expect an immediate response to a first approach – it may understandably be met by a degree of suspicion – and periods of silence may well be part of the process, at least in the early stages. Few faith communities have the same organisational structures as our churches, and therefore finding the 'right' point of contact may take some time. Hindus are attempting to become more 'Wester-nised' in their structures, but this is not necessarily true of all faith groups. Western converts to another faith, while they may seem a ready point of contact, are not always the best people from whom to seek an initial response.

In the light of this, an ideal first approach would be through someone known to the church. It is impossible to over-estimate the value of personal contact, and even where a 'cold call' letter has to be the first step, a follow-up visit or phone call could be pivotal. Civic backing for an inter-faith initiative is also important, and therefore the local authority and any local racial equality council should be made aware of developments at an early stage. Local authorities now look to consult closely with faith communities – pursuing some of their statutory duties actually requires them to do this – and many are also committed to working to deepen community cohesion. Hence these authorities have more than a passing interest in the existence of multi-faith bodies. Local Strategic Partnerships, which exist to bring public, private, community and voluntary sectors together to ensure the effectiveness of local public services, will also often seek to draw in the local inter-faith body.

Once trust begins to be built up and the process starts to move, the business of deciding on a name, structure, programme of events, source of financial support, criteria for membership and other key issues can be addressed. *The Local Inter Faith Guide* is helpful in setting out the factors to be considered at each stage and offering advice and practical guidance, not least in the area of providing food for an inter-faith event. The guide also explains the role of regional faith forums and the value of local inter-faith bodies being in contact with them.

Local factors, individual personalities and the dynamic that develops between the different groups and people involved will help to shape the group's activities and goals, and no two networks will be identical. While there is a broad framework within which they should operate, there is no 'blueprint' for an inter-faith forum or council. But whatever form such a council or group takes, it is important that at the heart of its work remains a shared commitment to deepen trust and friendship between the different faith groups in our communities as a step towards building a more just and peaceful society.

Keeping the faith

It needs to be stressed that inter-faith work is not, as some critics have maintained, about watering down one's faith in order to find some 'big consensus', nor is it about seeking to remove Christmas and other distinctively Christian festivals from the calendar and replacing them with 'less offensive' alternatives like a 'Winter Festival'! The idea that people of one faith are 'offended' by the outward manifestations of another faith is promulgated more by secular commentators and bodies than by people of faith themselves (and may be part of a more sinister agenda to force faith out of the public square). In fact, dialogue between different faiths can only be truly effective when those participating are sure of their doctrines and prepared to express and explain them with confidence. Inter-faith work is built upon a mutual respect for others' beliefs, traditions and scriptures, and is most effectively taken forward by those who, while open to genuine dialogue and a search for shared values, are firmly rooted in their own tradition. A metaphor from the Book of Isaiah – cited in the *Faithful Cities* report – is particularly apposite in this context: when lengthening the ropes of your tent, make sure that you also strengthen its pegs (Isa. 54:2).[14]

The idea that interaction with other faiths is only justified if it leads to opportunities to proselytise is also heard in some Christian circles, and while we are clearly called to preach the Gospel in and out of season, we must be clear that evangelism and inter-faith work should never be confused. Seeking friendship with and a better understanding of people of other faiths is both valid and worthwhile in its own right, and not only does it need no further justification, but it would be summarily and irrevocably derailed were it ever to be used as a 'Trojan horse' for outreach or any other hidden agenda.

Inter-faith action

If dialogue and conversation are vital ways of bringing our different faith traditions closer together, working side by side on community-based projects can take the relationship to an even deeper level. We noted in an earlier chapter the opportunities that exist for churches to contribute to the regeneration of their neighbourhoods, and where other faith traditions are similarly rooted in a local community and concerned for its well-being, there is potential for involvement in joint projects across faith boundaries. As with church-based community projects, there are many factors to consider, not least the availability of funding and the 'target-based' conditions that may be attached to it, though funding can sometimes be more readily forthcoming where a project is 'multi-faith' and not owned simply by a church or a council of churches. Faiths working together may also be in a stronger position to argue for a better deal for their project, and should not be afraid to do so. As a report produced by the London Churches Group for Social Action and Greater London Enterprise in 2002 observed, faith groups will sometimes need to 'challenge policy makers who see short-term goals as being sufficient' and 'should be willing to use their status to deliver forthright views on the need for sustainability and long term funding.'[15]

Faith groups will also want to increase awareness among statutory bodies of the role that faith plays in giving communities an identity and motivating people to engage in social action, of how their agenda might extend beyond that of simply another 'service provider'. The increasing involvement by the 'faith sector' in neighbourhood regeneration has caught some central and local government bodies unprepared, and often these bodies display considerable ignorance (which can, sadly, lead to prejudice) about the ethos and traditions of faith communities and what drives them to social action. One inter-faith organisation which set out to tackle this problem was Suffolk Inter-Faith Resource, which hosted a major conference entitled 'Issues of Identity, Faith and Culture' for 150 representatives of the faith communities in the county and people working in various government agencies. Following the success of this, Suffolk Inter-Faith Resource was invited to deliver ongoing lunch-time seminars on the faiths for County Council staff and local authority employees in other Suffolk towns.

One thing about which we need to convince funding bodies and government at local and national level is the value of 'faith' as a category (alongside, for example, 'race' and 'culture'). As Joy Madeiros, Faithworks' Director of Public Policy, has put it, faith is 'an integral part of society that is vital to community cohesion'. Madeiros suggests that, while 'government has championed the *role* and *work* of faith communities, the *faith* of faith communities appears not to be so welcome, particularly in so far as it relates to public funding' and that therefore 'there is a great deal of confusion at the local level about whether groups, motivated by their faith to serve others in communities, can be funded.' One reason for this confusion is an assumption by some funding bodies that when, for example, a project claims the identity of a particular faith, it cannot possibly be committed to serving all people regardless of their religious beliefs, ethnicity, sexual orientation and so on. By being committed to working in a manner that is professional, inclusive, transparent and accountable, we can begin to show the fallacy of this belief and demonstrate that faith groups *can* be trusted to deliver a good community service.[16]

It is easy to speak of 'faith communities' as one strand within the 'third sector', and government agencies and commentators often do this, but we also need to be sensitive to the unevenness of the power relationships that may develop between ourselves, as churches, and other communities as we engage in regeneration projects. As the report *'Faith' in urban regeneration?* noted, Christianity – and particularly the Church of England – still has a privileged status in this country and white-majority churches will, on the whole, be better resourced, have better contacts and have more experience of engagement in public regeneration policy and practice than other faith communities and black-majority churches. As the report says, 'these inequalities must be recognised and addressed if there is to be genuine engagement with the fullest range of faith communities and organisations.'[17] There will be exceptions to this, of course, and in some cases churches find themselves in a *less* equal position in terms of resources as funding bodies make a preferential option for other faiths precisely because they are minorities. Some funding officers may even need convincing that being 'Christian' is a religious identity as much as being Sikh or Hindu and deserving of equal treatment in funding terms.

Faith-based projects can be effective in terms of both changing the lives of individuals and communities and bringing people of different faith traditions and cultures closer together. Operation Eden in Liverpool is one example: initiated by the Anglican Diocese and funded by several regional and national bodies, it encourages local faith communities to engage in environmental projects which will be beneficial to the community, and supports them with small-scale funding, training and advice. Concern for the environment is common to all the major faiths, and through this partnership they have generated more than 100 projects around recycling, renewable energy, food growing and education, including the construction of an outdoor classroom for primary school children. Employment Focus, formerly Employment Forum UK, is another influential project with a strong multi-faith dimension. Founded in 1999 by Anglican priest Chris Beales, it runs programmes across the country which equip people from minority ethnic communities, including refugees and asylum seekers, with the necessary skills to enable them to find gainful employment.

Other examples abound. In Coventry a community centre was opened in 2006 with a Sikh as general manager and a Christian minister as chair. The building houses a centre for refugee support and provides space for Muslim women to meet and a black-majority church to worship. The project also offers a 'choice-based' local lettings scheme for affordable housing. In a Muslim-majority area of Birmingham an Anglican church hall houses a pre-school nursery, an after-school club, a family support service and a facility for mums and toddlers, all of which are open to and staffed by members of all faiths. In Plymouth a multi-faith event to highlight the plight of asylum seekers led to the emergence of a project to provide short-term accommodation, advice and other assistance to seekers in the city. And in London faith communities are coming together to discuss the implications of the 2012 Olympic Games being held in the city and how they can contribute to their success and ensure local communities benefit through regeneration.

As churches within a fragmenting and increasingly fearful society, we would do well to reflect on whether we are currently part of the problem or part of the solution – and commit to being part of the latter. Though inter-faith work is never 'easy', working together as people of different faiths in a spirit of mutual respect and with a shared concern for the well-being of our communities can be immensely rewarding. It can also help develop strong and lasting bridges between our different communities and make a significant contribution to the search for a more inclusive and cohesive society. Not least it can inspire us to deepen and develop our own faith for, as Birmingham-based Sikh leader Bhai Sahib Ji has put it, 'sometimes, if you want to regenerate the community, you must start by regenerating the faith'.[18]

Dialogue in the community

Churches in good standing in their communities can promote dialogue in other ways. A church not having a committed position on a particular local or regional issue can play a valuable role in bringing to the table the different parties concerned to enable views to be heard, differences resolved and the process moved forward. The *Faithful Cities* report calls on churches to help establish regular forums or consultations with young people as one way of enabling their views to help inform the local decision-making process,[19] and pursuing initiatives focusing on particular local concerns – for example, anti-social behaviour or the provision of local services – involving other sections of the community is a valuable contribution churches can make to the communities they serve.

One consequence of our modern propensity to 'narrowcast' is that movement on important issues at local, national and even global level can sometimes be hampered by the failure of those involved to communicate with each other. NGOs, official bodies, businesses, grassroots organisations, faith organisations and others can have a tendency often to shout past each other and critique each other's position without engaging face to face, which is not only counterproductive but can result in an impasse or even civic unrest and protest. There is a profoundly important place for protest, public criticism and even prophetic utterance, but the value of dialogue as an 'antidote to violence' should not be overlooked; often, in the long run, dialogue can achieve more than protest. An example of how this can work is provided by an event hosted by the United Reformed Church in November 2002, which although convened in response to an issue in a developing-world country, can be a model with wider application.

Concerned that, within the process of water-sector reform in Ghana (a country with which the URC has important links) too little space was being created for meaningful dialogue and too little information was being exchanged, the URC's Church and Society Committee, with the help of the head of a Ghanaian NGO and another development activist, facilitated a 24-hour 'round-table' near London. Invitations were issued to the Government of Ghana, the Trades Union Congress of Ghana, the World Bank, the UK Department for International Development, a private company interested in bidding for the water franchise and key NGOs from Ghana, the UK, the USA and the continent of Europe. The aim of the seminar was simply to encourage all these stakeholders to engage in dialogue with each other, not with the intent of winning arguments or point-scoring, but, in a spirit of mutual trust and respect, to understand one another's position and seek points of convergence from which the process could move forward.

That all the invitees attended the event – with the exception of the minister from the Government of Ghana who was prevented at the last minute by a crisis in the parliament – was due in large part to the fact that it was hosted by a church, which could make the credible claim that it was convening it in the interest of promoting dialogue and the search for a just settlement rather than the cause of any one particular stakeholder. And it was of great encouragement to the church that, not only did a spirit of cordiality and trust emerge and deepen as participants related to one another increasingly as people and less as simply agents of faceless institutions, but the process of water-sector reform in Ghana moved on as a consequence. A vital channel of communication opened up between the Government of Ghana, the TUC, the NGOs and the interested companies following this initiative, and a follow-up event was held in Accra the following year. Securing the trust of all participants in such an event will not always be easy, and this event nearly came unstuck when one of the participants discovered the URC's support for an NGO which had been critical of it and questioned how far a 'level playing field' would be operating. But the value of bringing together for sustained engagement (and social interaction) representatives of institutions with vastly different interests and perspectives, to find convergence around a potentially explosive issue which in another developing country had led to widespread unrest and the shooting of demonstrators, was palpable.

Another initiative through which churches and Christian agencies seek to use dialogue, in this case to engage the City of London over issues of global poverty and injustice, is 'JustShare'. While it began as a movement concerned to create space for peaceful protest in the City of London on May Day – at a time when anti-globalisation demonstrations on that day were becoming increasingly violent and self-defeating – JustShare has found value over time in developing conversations with institutions and people in the City through seminars, debates, boardroom meetings and even worship services. Its regular public debates provide opportunities for City people to discuss topics of current concern with leading figures from business, politics, the media, the Church and NGOs, and JustShare also reaches very senior decision-makers through events specially designed for them. JustShare remains committed to the value of protest and street action – in recent years, for example, it has held a rally on the steps of the Royal Exchange on May Day featuring a 'sermon for the City' given by a well-known church leader – and sees that as giving a vital edginess and unpredictability to its work. But it also argues that the message is sometimes more clearly and effectively communicated through conversation and dialogue conducted 'inside' the citadel than via a megaphone on the outside.

Epilogue

Let no one be discouraged by the belief there is nothing one man or one woman can do against the enormous array of the world's ills – against misery and ignorance, injustice and violence ... Few will have the greatness to bend history itself; but each of us can work to change a small portion of events, and in the total of all those acts will be written the history of this generation ...

It is from the numberless diverse acts of courage and belief that human history is shaped. Each time a person stands up for an ideal, or acts to improve the lot of others, or strikes out against injustice, they send a tiny ripple of hope, and crossing each other from a million different centres of energy and daring, those ripples build a current which can sweep down the mightiest walls of oppression and resistance.

Robert F. Kennedy
(address on the Day of Affirmation, University of Capetown,
South Africa, 6 June 1966; cited in Jeffrey Sachs,
The End of Poverty, London, 2005, pp. 367–8)

A Social Justice Calendar

January
- Peace Sunday (www.paxchristi.org.uk)
- Week of Prayer for Christian Unity (www.ctbi.org.uk)
- Holocaust Memorial Day (www.holocaustmemorialday.gov.uk)
- Homelessness Sunday (www.homelessness-sunday.org.uk)

February
- Poverty Action Sunday (www.church-poverty.org.uk/resources)
- Diocesan Lent appeals
- Anniversary of assassination of Janani Luwum
- Fairtrade Fortnight (www.fairtrade.org.uk)

March
- Women's World Day of Prayer (www.wwdp-natcomm.org)
- Anniversary of assassination of Oscar Romero (www.cafod.org.uk)

May
- Christian Aid Week (www.christianaid.org.uk)
- World Debt Day (www.jubileedebtcampaign.org.uk)
- World Fair Trade Day (www.wftday.org)

June
- Environment Sunday (formerly Conservation Sunday) (www.arocha.org)
- Refugee Week (www.refugeeweek.org.uk)

July
- National Justice & Peace Conference (www.justice-and-peace.org.uk)

August
- Anniversaries of Hiroshima & Nagasaki
  (www.paxchristi.org.uk / www.cnduk.org)

September
- Racial Justice Sunday (www.ctbi.org.uk/ccrj)
- Global Cease Fire Day (www.peaceoneday.org)

October
- CAFOD Harvest Fast Day (www.cafod.org.uk)
- International Day for Eradication of Poverty (www.un.org)
- One World Week (www.oneworldweek.org)
- Interfaith Week of Prayer for World Peace (nfpb.gn.apc.org)
- United Nations Day (www.un.org)
- Landmine Action Week (www.landmineaction.org)

November
- Remembrance Day
- Prisoners' Sunday (www.prisonsweek.org)
- Prisons Week (www.prisonsweek.org)

December
- Prisoners for Peace Day (www.wri-irg.org)
- World Aids Day (www.nat.org.uk)
- World Migration Day (www.ncrf.fsnet.co.uk)
- UN Human Rights Day (www.un.org)

Notes

Chapter 1: Introduction

1. David McKittrick, 'Their aim? Reconciliation. Their means? Talking', *The Independent*, 29 November 2006, pp. 2–3.
2. There are several excellent books in print arguing the case for Christians 'getting involved' and that authentic Christian witness involves social action; these include Jonathan Bartley, *Subversive Manifesto: Lifting the lid on God's political agenda*, Oxford: The Bible Reading Fellowship, 2003; and Malcolm Duncan, *Building a Better World: Faith at work for change in society*, London: Continuum, 2006. Interestingly, both have forewords by Steve Chalke.
3. Gerrard Winstanley, *A Watch-Word to the City of London and the Armie* (1649), cited in Andrew Bradstock & Christopher Rowland, eds., *Radical Christian Writings: A Reader*, Oxford: Blackwell, p. 132. The Diggers were a radical politico-religious movement in the time of Cromwell.
4. An example of the importance of being prepared to accept compromise is given by Conservative MP Ann Widdecombe: when confronted with a Bill which would not outlaw abortions but would prevent them being carried out in 92 per cent of cases, she voted in favour on the grounds that, if confronted with a shipwreck and 100 drowning people, she would not refuse to save 92 for the sake of 8; Archbishop Worlock Memorial Lecture 2006, cited in Nick Spencer, *Doing God: A Future for Faith in the Public Square*, London: Theos, 2006, p. 23.
5. See, for example, Deut. 15:4–5, where God suggests that if the people follow 'jubilee' principles 'there will be no more poor among you'. The apparently incompatible saying in Mark 14:7, 'the poor you will always have with you', could well be understood as Jesus telling his disciples that, if they remain faithful to him, then, yes, poor people will be the ones they spend most time with; cf. Jim Wallis, *God's Politics: Why the American Right Gets It Wrong and the Left Doesn't Get It*, Oxford: Lion Hudson, 2006, pp. 209f.
6. Though, as Jonathan Bartley has pointed out, church pressure did force members of the government into using the language of 'just war' to justify the invasion; *Faith and Politics After Christendom*, Milton Keynes: Paternoster, 2006, p. 138.
7. See, for example, Wallis, *God's Politics*, op. cit., Part I, pp. 3–40. While the thesis of this book is that change is achieved as popular pressure is applied to policy-makers and opinion-formers, this is not to ignore the fact that some key decisions are taken in arenas that some people deem not to be political; for example, the rise of the new public management has given new and striking influence and control to those who lead in the public sector in a manner which is qualitatively different to the period before the mid-1970s.
8. An aide at the summit is alleged to have heard one of the G8 leaders say, on surveying the demonstrators through a window, 'We're going to have to take this lot seriously – they're all priests'!
9. Ed Newell and Sabina Alkire's *What Can One Person Do?* (London: Darton Longman & Todd, 2005), is the perfect antidote to any feelings of impotence induced by the question it seeks to address!

10. See, for example, Isa. 1:12–17; 58:6–7; Hos. 6:6; Amos 5:21–4.
11. David Bosch, *Transforming Mission*, New York: Orbis, 1991.
12. Ann Morisy, *Journeying Out: A New Approach to Christian Mission*, London: Morehouse, 2004, p. 5.
13. Stuart Murray, *Post-Christendom: Church and mission in a strange new world*, Carlisle: Paternoster, 2004, pp. 19, 86, 248.
14. Walter Wink, *Engaging the Powers*, New York: Fortress, 1992.

Chapter 2: **War and Terror**

 1. A recent excellent discussion of this is Simon Barrow and Jonathan Bartley, eds., *Consuming Passion: Why the killing of Jesus really matters*, London: Darton, Longman & Todd, 2005.
 2. See, for example, the 'Church Order' set down by Hippolytus in AD 218, in Eberhard Arnold, *The Early Christians in Their Own Words*, Farmington & Robertsbridge: Plough, rev. edn 1997, pp. 113–14.
 3. While I acknowledge that the concept of the 'Just War' is still valued in sections of the Church which believe that violence can in certain circumstances be sanctioned, the purpose of this chapter is to look at the practicalities of conflict resolution rather than rehearse the arguments in the 'just war v. pacifism' debate. A premise of this chapter is that armed force cannot lead to true and lasting peace and that non-violence must seek to answer the questions that violence purports to answer but in a better way.
 4. Jim Wallis, *God's Politics: Why the American Right Gets It Wrong and the Left Doesn't Get It*, Oxford: Lion, 2005, p. 54.
 5. Clare Short, *An Honourable Deception? New Labour, Iraq and the Misuse of Power*, London: Simon & Schuster, 2004, p. 228.
 6. Wallis, op. cit., p. 171. See also Sydney Bailey, *Peace is a Process*, London: Quaker Home Service, 1993.
 7. 'Countering Terrorism: Power, Violence and Democracy Post 9/11', a report by a Working Group of the Church of England's House of Bishops, 2005, p. 75.
 8. This is not the place for an analysis of the distinction made within the discipline of peace studies between 'direct', 'structural' and 'cultural' violence, though it is helpful in enabling us to see how we might ourselves be responsible for inhibiting peace while also seeking to promote it.
 9. Diana Mavunduse and Simon Oxley, *Why Violence? Why not peace?*, Geneva: World Council of Churches, 2002, p. 5. This booklet also offers helpful ideas, discussion material and biblical reflection to help churches engage in peace-making.
10. Scilla Elworthy and Gabrielle Rifkind, *Making Terrorism History*, London: Random House, new rev. edn 2006, pp. 9–10.
11. Ibid., p. 27.
12. CND flyer, 2006.
13. Rachel Harden, ' "Replacing Trident would be anti-God act" say bishops', *Church Times*, 14 July 2006; Michael Bartlet, 'Making Good our NPT commitments', *The Friend*, 7 April 2006. Bartlet's interpretation is admittedly a highly contested one.
14. 'Countering Terrorism', op. cit., pp. 29–32.
15. Pat Gaffney, 'Blessed peacemakers', *The Tablet*, 1 April 2006, p. 10.
16. Elworthy and Rifkind, op. cit., p. 27.
17. Steve Hucklesby and Philip Woods, eds., 'Peacemaking: A Christian Vocation', the United Reformed Church and the Methodist Church, 2006, pp. 54–5.
18. 'Countering Terrorism', op. cit., p. 9; 'The Solution to Terrorism', *The Tablet*, 16 September 2006, p. 2. In April 2007 the then International Development Secretary,

Hilary Benn, announced that the UK government would cease using the term 'war on terror'.

19. Michael Northcott, *An Angel Directs the Storm: Apocalyptic Religion and American Empire*, London: I. B. Tauris, 2004, pp. 75, 110; cf. 'Countering terrorism', op. cit., pp. 47–8.
20. 'Countering terrorism', op. cit., p. 14.
21. Marcus Braybrook, 'The War Against Terror: The Interfaith alternative', *Church of England Newspaper*, 24 February 2006, p. 10.
22. Walter Wink, *Engaging the Powers: Discernment and Resistance in a World of Domination*, Minneapolis: Fortress Press, 1992, pp. 186–7.
23. Donald Reeves, 'The Moral Imagination', lecture at Lambeth Palace, 18 May 2006 (www.soulofeurope.org/articles/moralimagination.htm); see also Reeves, 'How mediation can heal the schism', *Church Times*, 26 January 2007, p. 9.
24. Professor Kember has since written up his experiences in *Hostage in Iraq*, London: Darton, Longman and Todd, 2007.
25. Kathleen Lonsdale, 'Removing the Causes of War', 1953 Swarthmore Lecture, London: George Allen & Unwin, 1953 (also available at http://Kingston.quaker.ca/quotes.htm).
26. And even fewer of us, I guess, will feel able to emulate the quite remarkable commitment of Brian Haw, who has maintained a permanent 24/7 protest vigil opposite the Houses of Parliament since the invasion of Iraq in March 2003.

Chapter 3: Climate Change

1. See, for example, Lynn White Jr, 'The Historical Roots of Our Ecologic(al) Crisis', *Science*, 155, 3767, 10 March 1967, pp. 1203–7; Max Nicholson, *The Environmental Revolution*, London: Hodder & Stoughton, 1969. For a useful short discussion of these attacks see Tim Cooper, *Green Christianity: Caring for the whole creation*, London: Hodder & Stoughton, 1990, pp. 33f.
2. This is not to ignore the influence of others who have provided Christianity with an environmentally friendly ethic, such as Hildegarde of Bingen, Bridget of Kildare and Francis of Assisi.
3. Jürgen Moltmann, *God in Creation*, London: SCM, 1985, p. 6; cited in Cooper, op. cit., p. 59.
4. 'Evangelicals launch green action plan', *The Guardian*, 9 February 2006.
5. The Fourth Assessment Report of the United Nations Intergovernmental Panel on Climate Change, published in early 2007, which said that global warming will happen faster and be more devastating than previously thought, provides a good summation of the views of world experts in the subject.
6. Mayer Hillman, *How We Can Save the Planet*, London: Penguin, 2004; Ruth Valerio, *L is for Lifestyle: Christian living that doesn't cost the earth*, Leicester: IVP, 2004.
7. CEL also runs a sustainable food and farming campaign promoting the 'LOAF' principles: Locally produced, Organically grown, Animal friendly and Fairly traded.
8. Further information about 'nature-friendly' gardening may be found on www.english-nature.org.uk or www.wildaboutgardens.org
9. Some of these projects are cited in David Pickering, 'Nailing their "Green Colours" to the Mast . . .', *Ecotheology*, 9.1, 2004, pp. 124–8.
10. Oliver James, *Affluenza: How to Be Successful and Stay Sane*, London: Vermillion, 2006.
11. Edward Echlin, article in *Catholic Gazette*, June 1989, cited in Cooper, op. cit, p. 256.

12. See, for example, James Jones, *Jesus and the Earth*, London: SPCK, 2003.
13. Paul Bodenham, 'Operation Noah – The Community Climate Change Campaign', *Ecotheology*, 10.1, 2005, p. 109.
14. *The climate of poverty: facts, fears and hope*, Christian Aid, 2006, pp. 1–2, 41.
15. Ibid., p. 41.
16. Colin Challen, 'Holidays in the sun: aviation's con trick', *Tribune*, 5 August 2005, pp. 14–15. Other politicians noted for their outspokenness on environmental issues are John Gummer and Michael Meacher.
17. Rowan Williams, 'Changing the myths we live by', lecture delivered at Lambeth Palace, 5 July 2004; Claire Foster, *Sharing God's Planet: a Christian vision for a sustainable future*, London: Church House Publishing, 2005, pp. 35–6.
18. David Adam & Rob Evans, 'Industry's enormous impact on climate revealed', *Guardian Weekly*, 19–25 May 2006, p. 9.
19. Williams, 'Changing the myths . . .', op. cit.
20. Michael Northcott, *A Moral Climate: The Ethics of Global Warming*, London: Darton, Longman & Todd, 2007. Northcott employs the concept of the mystical body of Christ to remind us of the obligations we have to Christians in other parts of the world who may be suffering from famine or other kinds of need.
21. Valerio, op. cit., p. 45.
22. Madeleine Bunting, 'Put us all on rations', *The Guardian*, 26 August 2004.
23. Andrew Simms, 'Our best is not enough', *The Guardian*, 13 December 2005.
24. Ashok Sinha, 'Just a question of will?', *The Common Good*, 192, 2005, p. 9.
25. Andrew Rawnsley, 'So now green is the new blue – and also the new red', *The Observer*, 23 April 2006.

Chapter 4: Make Poverty History

1. Speech at the Christian Socialist Movement's 'Faith in Politics' event, London, 2001.
2. Will Hutton, 'Debt-relief campaign Jubilee 2000 can now claim its great victory, thanks to Leviticus', *The Observer*, 3 October 1999.
3. See, for example, Clare Short, speech to the Assembly of the United Reformed Church, Portsmouth, July 2003 (http://hotline2003.urc.org.uk/content/clare-short-full.htm).
4. Geraldine Bedell, *Make Poverty History: How You Can Help Defeat World Poverty in Seven Easy Steps*, London: Penguin, 2005, p. 30.
5. Speech delivered in February 2004, cited in Sabina Alkire and Edmund Newell, *What Can One Person Do? Faith to Heal a Broken World*, London: Darton, Longman & Todd, 2005, p. 32. A major breakthrough occurred in the 'currency tax' campaign in May 2007 when the specialist finance company INTL Global Currencies successfully trialled a 0.005% levy on its trades for a week.
6. Jenny Ricks, 'We need trade justice to make poverty history', *One World Week Newsletter*, 2005, p. 1.
7. Bedell, op. cit., p. 11.
8. Tearfund, *Feeling the Heat*, 2006; Christian Aid, *The Climate of Poverty: facts, fears and hope*, 2006.
9. Wilf Wilde, *Crossing the River of Fire*, London: Epworth, 2006, p. 19.
10. Larry Elliott, 'Gleneagles did not short-change Africa', *The Guardian*, 3 July 2006, p. 26.
11. Paul Vallely, 'Not just one brief, shining moment', *The Tablet*, 1 July 2006, p. 7.
12. *The Guardian 'G2'*, 28 December 2005, p. 5. One of the best reflections on Gleneagles – what the agencies demanded, what the G8 leaders promised, what has

happened since and how churches might respond – is Stephen Rand, 'Poverty isn't history yet', *Church Times*, 6 January 2006, pp. 16–17.

13. See, for example, Annie Kelly, 'Ready for a place at the top tables', *The Guardian Weekly*, 26 January 2007.

14. Vallely, op. cit., p. 6.

15. To sign the Micah Call visit www.micahchallenge.org

Chapter 5: Make Poverty History Here

1. For example, Archbishop John Sentamu called on Christians to 'challenge poverty' in an open letter during the re-launch of the Church Urban Fund in June 2006; *Faithful Cities: A call for celebration, vision and justice* (Methodist Publishing House and Church House Publishing, 2006) reminded churches of their 'duty to challenge the thoughtless accumulation of wealth which ignores the needs of the poor, both globally and locally' (p. 90); the report of the Fabian Society's Commission on Life Chances and Child Poverty, *Narrowing the Gap*, called for a 'coalition to eliminate UK poverty on a similar scale to that mobilised by Make Poverty History' (pp. 4, 207); and David Lammy MP (with public endorsement by Chancellor of the Exchequer Gordon Brown) encouraged churches to pursue a similar goal in a Christian Socialist Movement / Von Hügel Institute pamphlet (David Lammy, *Make Poverty History Here*, London: CSM/VHI, 2006). Ed Balls MP also called for a cross-party, all-faith coalition in a speech to the End Child Poverty group in October 2005 (*The Guardian*, 18 October 2005).

2. Jonathan Sacks, 'Thought for the Day', BBC Radio 4, 8 December 2006.

3. Mark Gould, 'Poor understanding', *Society Guardian*, 7 June 2006, p. 5.

4. *Narrowing the Gap*, op. cit., p. 33.

5. 'Poor understanding', op. cit.

6. *Narrowing the Gap*, op. cit., pp. 29–30.

7. *Narrowing the Gap*, op. cit., *passim*.

8. Letter to *Church Times*, 6 October 2006.

9. These stories come from Paul Nicolson, 'Poverty: the cost to families', *The Tablet*, 2 December 2006, p. 4.

10. Niall Cooper, 'Hapless, helpless or shameless', *Christian Socialist*, 190, Spring 2005, p. 10.

11. John Veit-Wilson, 'Can poverty be abolished?', *Church Action on Poverty News*, Autumn 2005, p. 9.

12. 'Poor understanding', op. cit., p. 5.

13. Catherine Howarth & Bob Holman, 'Getting angry again ...', *Christian Socialist*, 190, Spring 2005, pp. 7–8; Bob Holman, 'Poverty, a practical response: what will the Blairs do next?', in Faithworks, ed., *Poor Relations*, London: 2006, pp. 7–11.

14. Richard Wilkinson, *The Impact of Inequality: how to make sick societies healthier*, London: Routledge, 2005.

15. Sue Regan & Peter Robinson, *Overcoming Disadvantage: An agenda for the next twenty years*, York: Joseph Rowntree Foundation, 2004, p. 14, cited in *Faithful Cities*, op. cit., p. 33.

16. Stewart Lansley, 'The super rich', Compass Thinkpiece 8, 2006. See also Michael Schluter, 'Pay Differentials and Relationships', *Engage*, 15, Winter 2006, p. 2.

17. *Faithful Cities*, op. cit., p. 35. The report also supported a 'living' rather than a 'minimum' wage (p. 90).

18. *The Guardian*, 4 March 2005, cited in Jennifer Swift, 'Bidding to break the shackles of debt', *The Church of England Newspaper*, 5 May 2006, p. 9.

19. Ann Pettifor, *The Coming First World Debt Crisis*, London: Palgrave Macmillan, 2006.

20. Maeve Sherlock, 'Destitution by design', *Church Action on Poverty News*, Spring 2006, p. 4.
21. One attempt to make known the 'real life' experiences of people seeking asylum in the UK is Andrew Bradstock & Arlington Trotman, eds., *Asylum Voices*, London: CTBI, 2003.
22. Francis Davis, Jolanta Stankeviciute, David Ebbutt & Robert Kaggwa, *The Ground of Justice: The report of a pastoral research enquiry into the needs of migrants in London's Catholic community*, Cambridge: Von Hügel Institute, 2007 (downloadable at www.vhi.org.uk).
23. Steve Chalke, *Faithworks Unpacked: a practical manual to equip churches for community involvement*, Eastbourne: Kingsway, 2003, p. 22.
24. Phil Jump, *Community Regeneration and Neighbourhood Renewal: Towards a Baptist Response*, Didcot: Baptist Union of Great Britain, 2001, p. 5.
25. On 'social capital' see, for example, Ann Morisy, *Journeying Out: A new approach to Christian Mission*, London: Morehouse, 2004, ch. 3; and Chris Baker & Hannah Skinner, *Telling the Stories: How churches are contributing to social capital*, Manchester: William Temple Foundation, 2004; on 'faithful capital' see *Faithful Cities*, op. cit., pp. 2–4.
26. Two reports produced by the Northwest Development Agency in 2003 and 2005 identified more than 5000 significant 'non-worship' projects undertaken by faith communities in that region alone, involving more than 45,000 volunteers working 8.1 million volunteer hours per annum – the equivalent of 4815 full-time jobs; Nick Spencer, *Doing God: A Future for Faith in the Public Square*, London: Theos, 2006, p. 43.
27. Spencer, op. cit., p. 69.
28. Diocese of Liverpool website (http://liverpool.anglican.org/people/bishops/bishopjamesindex.htm).
29. Tim Lawrence, *In Search of Living Waters: An introduction to community development from a Christian perspective*, London: Shaftesbury Society, 2005, pp. 10–11.
30. Spencer, op. cit., pp. 52–3.
31. Ann Pettifor, 'Towards Economic Transformation: the role of the churches' in Andrew Bradstock & Paul Murray, eds., *Global Capitalism and the Gospel of Justice: Politics, economics and the UK churches* (papers from the Ushaw Conference, July 2001), 2003, pp. 14–15; cf. *Faithful Cities*, op. cit., pp. 77–8.
32. Francis Davis, *Faith in Social Enterprise: A call to the churches and the nation*, London: Christian Socialist Movement, 2006, p. 10.
33. Steve Chalke, *Faithworks*, Eastbourne: Kingsway, 2001, p. 55.

Chapter 6: Faith and Fear

1. Jonathan Sacks, *The Dignity of Difference: How to avoid the clash of civilisations*, London: Continuum, rev. edn, 2003, p. 2.
2. Ibid.
3. *Faithful Cities: A call for celebration, vision and justice*, Methodist Publishing House and Church House Publishing, 2006, pp. 23–5.
4. *Daily Telegraph*, 9 July 2005, cited in Milan Rai, *7/7: The London bombings, Islam and the Iraq war*, London: Pluto Press, 2006, p. 59; Joe Murphy, 'Muslims feared on the Tube since 7/7', *London Lite*, 5 September 2006, p. 8.
5. Leslie Griffiths, *Multiculturalism: a shattered dream?*, London: CSM, 2005, p. 6.
6. A survey by the '1990 Trust' in 2006 found that between 1 and 2 per cent of Muslims believed acts of terrorism against civilians in the UK were justified – as compared to the 20 per cent found by some newspaper polls whose questions, the

trust suggested, might have been loaded to elicit highly charged responses. See Jonathan Freedland, *The Guardian*, 18 October, 2006, p. 31.
7. Rai, op. cit., ch. 10, pp. 69–76; cf. p. 156.
8. *The Tablet*, 14 October 2006, p. 19.
9. In private correspondence.
10. Kenneth Leech, *Race: Changing Society and the Churches*, London: SPCK, pp. 76–7, cited in *Faithful Cities*, op. cit., p. 26.
11. 'Looking after one another', Inter Faith Network for the UK, 2005. Available from 8A Lower Grosvenor Place, London SW1W 0EN.
12. Three Faiths Forum press release, 19 February 2006 (www.threefaithsforum.org.uk/PressReleases/19022006ActGoodwill.htm).
13. See, for example, Ramesh Kallidai, 'Listening to British Hindus', *The Common Good*, 191, Summer 2005, pp. 6–7.
14. *Faithful Cities*, op. cit., p. 75.
15. Terry Drummond, Elizabeth Simon, Madeleine Williams & Laurie Anderson, *Neighbourhood renewal in London: The role of faith communities*, London: Greater London Enterprise / London Churches Group, 2002, p. 20.
16. Joy Madeiros, 'Relating to Faith: A leadership challenge' in Faithworks, ed., *Poor Relations*, London: 2006, p. 15.
17. Richard Farnell, Robert Furbey, Stephen Shams, Al-Haqq Hills, Marie Macey & Greg Smith, *Faith in urban regeneration? Engaging faith communities in urban regeneration*, Bristol: Policy Press, 2003, p. 10.
18. Jonathan Gurling, 'Putting faith at the centre', *The Church of England Newspaper*, 1 September 2006, p. 19.
19. *Faithful Cities*, op. cit. p. 41.

Websites

Chapter 2
Decade to Overcome Violence – www.overcomingviolence.org
Oxford Research Group – www.oxfordresearchgroup.org.uk
Conscience: the peace tax campaign – www.conscienceonline.org.uk
Quaker House, Belfast – www.quakerhousebelfast.org
Corrymeela – www.corrymeela.org
Soul of Europe – www.soulofeurope.org
Christian Peacemaker Teams – www.cptuk.org.uk
Fellowship of Reconciliation – www.for.org.uk
Pax Christi – www.paxchristi.org.uk
University of Bradford Department of Peace Studies – www.bradford.ac.uk/acad/
peace

Chapter 3
Eco-Congregation – www.ecocongregation.org
Christian Ecology Link – www.christian-ecology.org.uk
Shrinking the Footprint – www.shrinkingthefootprint.cofe.anglican.org
A Rocha – www.arocha.org
Church of Scotland SRT project – www.srtp.org.uk
European Christian Environmental Network – www.ecen.org
Stop Climate Chaos – www.stopclimatechaos.org
Earth Charter – www.earthcharter.org
Friends of the Earth – www.foe.co.uk
Sustrans – www.sustrans.org.uk

Chapter 4
Trade Justice Movement – www.tjm.org.uk
Make Poverty History – www.makepovertyhistory.org
Jubilee Debt Campaign – www.jubileedebtcampaign.org.uk
Stamp Out Poverty – www.stampoutpoverty.org
Stop AIDS Campaign – www.stopaidscampaign.org.uk
Christian Aid – www.christian-aid.org
CAFOD – www.cafod.org.uk
Tearfund – www.tearfund.org
SCIAF – www.sciaf.org.uk
Fairtrade Foundation – www.fairtrade.org.uk
'livesimply' – www.livesimply.org.uk
Micah Challenge – www.micahchallenge.org
CRED (Fairtrade jewellery) – www.cred.tv
Speak – www.speak.org.uk
World Development Movement – www.wdm.org.uk
Traidcraft – www.traidcraft.org.uk

Chapter 5
Church Urban Fund – www.cuf.org.uk
Church Action on Poverty – www.church-poverty.org.uk
Zacchaeus 2000 Trust – www.z2k.org
Shaftesbury – www.shaftesburysoc.org.uk
Emmaus – www.emmaus.org.uk
Christians Against Poverty – www.capuk.org
End Child Poverty – www.endchildpoverty.org.uk
Child Poverty Action Group – www.cpag.org.uk
Credit Action – www.creditaction.org.uk
Hope 2008 – www.hope08.com
Refugee Council – www.refugeecouncil.org.uk
CHASTE – www.chaste.org.uk
Faithworks – www.faithworks.info
More Than Gold – www.morethangold.org.uk
Strangers into Citizens – www.strangersintocitizens.org.uk
Stop the Traffik – www.stopthetraffik.org

Chapter 6
Building Bridges Pendle – www.pendle.net/buildingbridges
St Philip's Centre – www.stphilipscentre.co.uk
St Ethelburga's – www.stethelburgas.org
Christian-Muslim Forum – www.christianmuslimforum.org
Faith Together in Leeds 11 – www.faithtogether.org.uk
Peacemakers – www.peacemakers.tv
The Council of Christians and Jews – www.ccj.org.uk
Operation Eden – www.operation-eden.org.uk
Employment Focus – www.employmentfocus.org
JustShare – www.justshare.org.uk

Reading and resources

Chapter 1

Atherton, John, *Public Theology for Changing Times*, London, 2000.
Bartley, Jonathan, *Subversive Manifesto*, Oxford, 2003.
Duncan, Malcolm, *Building a Better World*, London, 2006.
Gordon, Graham, *What If You Got Involved?* Carlisle, 2003.
Spencer, Nick, *Doing God: A Future for Faith in the Public Square*, London, 2006.
Stott, John, *Issues Facing Christians Today*, Grand Rapids, 4th edn, 2006.
Wallis, Jim, *God's Politics*, Oxford, 2005.
Evangelical Alliance, *Uniting for Change: an evangelical vision for transforming society*, n.d.
Change the World for a Fiver, London, 2004.

Chapter 2

Elworthy, Scilla & Rifkind, Gabrielle, *Making Terrorism History*, London, 2006.
Gidron, Benjamin, et al., *Mobilizing for Peace*, New York, 2002.
Griffiths, Leslie & Potter, Jennifer, *World Without End? Contours of a Post-Terrorism Landscape*, London, 2007.
Hucklesby, Steve & Woods, Philip, eds., *Peacemaking: A Christian Vocation*, London, 2006.
Kember, Norman, *Hostage in Iraq*, London, 2007.
Morris, Colin, *Things Shaken – Things Unshaken*, Peterborough, 2006.
Prout, Alison, *Tanks and Trolleys*, London, 2006.
Solly Megoran, Nick, *The War on Terror: How Should Christians Respond?*, Nottingham, 2007
Young, Jeremy, *The Violence of God and the War on Terror*, London, 2007.
House of Bishops, *Countering Terrorism: Power, Violence and Democracy Post 9/11*, 2005.

Chapter 3

Foster, Claire, *Sharing God's Planet: a Christian vision for a sustainable future*, London, 2005.
Foster, Claire & Shreeve, David, *How Many Lightbulbs Does it Take to Change a Christian?*, London, 2007.
Gore, Al, *An Inconvenient Truth*, New York, 2006.
Gorringe, Tim, *Harvest: Food, farming and the churches*, London, 2006.
McDonagh, Sean, *Living Lightly on the Earth*, London, 2004.
Monbiot, George, *Heat: How to stop the planet burning*, London: 2006.
Northcott, Michael, *A Moral Climate: The Ethics of Global Warming*, London, 2007.
Spencer, Nick, & White, Robert, *Christianity, Climate Change and Sustainable Living*, London, 2007.
Tillett, Sarah (ed.), *Caring for Creation*, London, 2006.

Valerio, Ruth, *L is for Lifestyle: Christian living that doesn't cost the earth*, Leicester, 2004.

Don't Throw It All Away: Friends of the Earth's Guide to reducing Waste, London, 2004

Chapter 4

Alkire, Sabina & Newell, Edmund, *What Can One Person Do?* London, 2005.
Bedell, Geraldine, *Make Poverty History*, London, 2005.
Curtis, Mark, *Trade for Life*, London, 2001.
Litvinoff, Miles & Madeley, John, *50 Reasons to Buy Fair Trade*, London, 2007.
Madeley, John, *Hungry for Trade*, London, 2000.
Madeley, John, *100 Ways to Make Poverty History*, London, 2005.
Northcott, Michael, *Life After Debt*, London, 1999.
Sachs, Jeffrey, *The End of Poverty*, London, 2005.
Wroe, Martin & Doney, Malcolm, *The Rough Guide to a Better World*, London, n.d.

Chapter 5

Faithful Cities: A call for celebration, vision and justice, London, 2006.
Chalke, Steve, *Faithworks Unpacked (3)*, Eastbourne, 2002.
Chalke, Steve & Watkins, Anthony, *100 Ways to Transform Your Community*, Eastbourne, 2003.
Fabian Commission on Life Chances and Child Poverty, *Narrowing the Gap*, London, 2006.
Finneron, Doreen et al., *Challenging Communities*, Durham & London, n.d.
Lammy, David, *Make Poverty History Here*, London, 2006.
Pettifor, Ann, *The Coming First World Debt Crisis*, London, 2006.
United Reformed Church, *Assets for Life* (resource pack & DVD), 2004.

Chapter 6

Faithful Cities: A call for celebration, vision and justice, London, 2006.
Inter Faith Network for the UK, *The Local Inter Faith Guide*, London, 2005.
The Methodist Church, *Faith Meeting Faith*, London, 2004.
Drummond, Terry, et al., *Neighbourhood renewal in London*, London, 2002.
Farnell, Robert, et al., *'Faith' in urban regeneration?*, Bristol, 2003.
Finneron, Doreen & Dinham, Adam, eds., *Building on Faith*, London, n.d.

Index

Index of Biblical References